JESUS IN THE GOSPELS

JESUS IN THE GOSPELS

Old Stories Told Anew

RICHARD MAZZIOTTA, C.S.C.

Ave Maria Press   Notre Dame, Indiana

Library of Congress Catalog Card Number: 86-70132

International Standard Book Number: 0-87793-336-7

Cover design: Elizabeth J. French

Photography:
Jagdish Agarwal, 107; Marne Breckensiek, 17; Ron Byers, 27; Paul Conklin, 47; John E. Fitzgerald, 171, 189; Bob & Miriam Francis, 179; Betty Hurwich-Zoss, 57, 161; Jean Claude Lejeune, 39; Robert Maust, cover, 97, 125; Rev. Patrick Mooney, 135; Bruce Roberts, 151; Joan Sauro, 71; Lee Snider, 81.

Printed and bound in the United States of America.

*To the Dominican Sisters
of St. Catharine, Kentucky
who first told these stories to me*

Acknowledgments

These stories were written during the fall of 1984. When I requested a semester sabbatical from responsibilities at Stonehill College, Bartley MacPháidín, president, encouraged me. Had he not so kindly granted this autumn leisure, this manuscript would not have been written.

I thank the Holy Cross community in North Dartmouth, Massachusetts — especially Margaret Coté, Joseph Morris, James F. Murphy and Laetus Triolo for welcoming me into their house for those important months. Near to both the resources of a university library and an Atlantic beach, I could not have chosen a more ideal setting.

I do not think that anyone ever read between the lines with more accuracy than did Denise LaBlanc, who over and over again updated scrawled upon manuscripts. Also for practical kindnesses at critical moments during this project and at other times, I thank Craig W. Binney.

My appreciation for theology and imagination has been deepened by the companionship of others. For this, it is time to thank my teachers, especially Eileen Maura Hourihan, Robert J. Kruse, Charles E. Sheedy and Elisabeth Schüssler Fiorenza.

Finally, I thank all who have been true friends to me — friends in time of need, especially Eugene Green, Douglas S. Gould and James R. Lackenmier.

Contents

Introduction

I

Storytelling, an art form once considered best reserved to the bedsides of little children, is now one that theologians and preachers seek to acquire. The more one thinks of this, the more valid as theological discourse storytelling seems. After all, for most Christians, their first holy communion with Christ occurred years before they approached the altar one May morning to receive the Eucharist. First holy communion with Christ occurs in storytelling, when, for example, parents bring small children to the table scene in a church on Christmas morning and tell the story of how on a cold, dark December night, God came upon the earth, was born of Mary and was visited by shepherds — and how sad it all was that for them there were no accommodations in the inn.

The legitimacy of storytelling as theological discourse becomes more apparent when its link to the human faculty of hearing is underscored. As a human faculty, hearing, of course, is primitive, more primitive, in fact, than vision.

It is likely that the sense of hearing developed to acuteness during the age when our ancestors lived outdoors in the night or dwelt in caves. In such a life, it was essential that one heard danger's approach before one saw it.

For the inner life of the soul, hearing is a critical faculty because it supports the eschatological dimension of faith that is directed toward the end of human history, the end of storytelling. In this sense, to hear is to wait.[1] We learn this from human discourse, where to listen to a speaker is simultaneously to wait for the end of the remarks. This is nowhere more obvious than in the telling of a joke. What makes the telling of a joke successful is first the establishment

---

[1] See F.J. van Beeck's *Christ Proclaimed* (N.Y.: Paulist Press, 1979), pp. 279-286, for a comprehensive treatment of this important theme.

and then the building of suspense as the joker unfolds the narrative before an audience. What is more excruciating than listening through the telling of a joke which was heard once already? Hence, there is that most courteous of questions, "Have you heard the one about . . .?"

To attend to the word of God is like waiting for the punch line of a joke. That is, for believers who participate in revelation, they wait for the last hour when, like a joker, God will speak that final and all-encompassing word which will impart meaning to all that has preceded and which will order and shape history in a way that will reveal at last its unity and plan.

II

The first preaching about Christ was in story form that employed wise use of landscape-seascape, character, politics, and plot. Peter's address on Pentecost Sunday demonstrates:

> I take it you know what has been reported all over Judea about Jesus of Nazareth, beginning in Galilee with the baptism John preached; of the way God anointed him with the Holy Spirit and with power. He went about doing good works and healing all who were in the grip of the devil, and God was with him. We are witnesses to all that he did in the land of the Jews and in Jerusalem. They killed him finally, "hanging him on a tree," only to have God raise him up on the third day and grant that he be seen, not by all, but only by such witnesses as had been chosen beforehand by God —by us who ate and drank with him after he rose from the dead (Ac 10:37-41 NAB).

Over the centuries this aspect of the gospel became subordinated to doctrinal and catechetical concerns of the church.

I developed this fashion of copying the gospel into stories somewhat by accident. In preaching I became convinced of the pastoral fruitfulness of retelling the gospel text of the day. The purpose of the stories of this volume is to assist modern-day believers in hearing the gospels anew as stories, however arduous that effort might be due to the frequency with which these familiar texts have been heard.

Since they are not biographies of Jesus but theological reflections of the primitive church, the gospels cannot provide full assistance to those who wish to understand the Jewish ethos, the political and material hardships and the richness of religious culture that defined Jesus, his kin and disciples as well as his adversaries of the Roman and religious establishments. These stories hope to satisfy this traditional interest of believers. When extended to the extreme, of course, such curiosity can become distorted, as is seen in exaggerated piety surrounding the veneration of relics. In its proper perspective, genuine interest in the life of Jesus can support the life of belief while doing no injustice to the crucial distinction made from the 19th century onwards between the historical Jesus and the Christ of faith.

III

I wrote above that I copy the gospel. I am not the first to have done this. Neither in theology nor in the arts is this original.

From their own rich tradition of Talmudic narrative, the Jewish authors of the apocryphal gospels composed stories of the life of Jesus to supplement the short supply of detail that the canonical gospels provided. Our age, though far removed in time from the theological concerns of the gospel writers, thanks to modern scholarship, is actually more able to reconstruct the life and times of Jesus than were the authors of the apocryphal gospels whose accounts seem to us rather far-fetched and untheological.

There is ample precedent for reinterpretation of this kind not only in theology, but also in the arts. To cite examples from literature: Shakespeare's *Comedy of Errors* copies Platus' play *Menaechmi*; Rogers' *Boys from Syracuse* became Sondheim's *A*

Funny Thing Happened on the Way to the Forum; and Sophocles' *Antigone* has been copied in Jean Anouihl's play of the same name. In another area, J.S. Bach's *Concerto in A Minor for Organ* is a reinterpretation of Vivaldi's concerto of the same name for orchestra.

Is there merit is such a method? Can the imagination be involved if the author has taken whole cloth the original inspiration of another? There is both artistic and personal value, I believe.

Though all are aware of Vincent van Gogh's creative genius, not all know that as an artist he frequently and without apology, copied the works of others. Writing to his brother Theo shortly before he died, Vincent lamented the impatience that demanded that painters be wholly original all the time. In the judgment of this artist, it was the authentic practice of art for a painter to interpret the original work of another. In his letter to Theo, Vincent defended not only the enjoyment and consolation he took in a series of paintings in which he copied the work of Delacroix and Millet, but also the learning that he received:

> In music if some person or other plays Beethoven, he adds his personal interpretation — in music and more especially in singing — the interpretation of a composer is something, and it is not a hard and fast rule that only the composer should play his own composition. . . . I let the black and white by Delacroix or Millet pose for me as a subject. And then I improvise color on it, not, you understand, altogether myself, but searching for memories of their pictures — but the memory, "the vague consonance of colors which are at least right in feeling" — that is my own interpretation.[2]

---

[2] V. van Gogh, *The Complete Letters* (Greenwich, Conn.: NY Graphic Society, 1959), III, Letter 607, p. 216.

IV

These stories of Jesus, these copies, are not historical in the exact sense of the word. No one can prove whether the priest Zechariah served as a mason during construction of the sanctuary of Herod's temple, that Joseph and Miriam traveled in a caravan to Bethlehem, or whether Joseph of Arimathaea raised his voice for the defense during the trial of Jesus before the Sanhedrin. Throughout, I have made every effort, first, to be certain that these details are plausible, that they could have happened; second, that all which has been written in these stories is faithful to what scholarship verifies concerning Jesus' life and times; and, third, and most importantly, that these stories are responsible to what biblical scholarship establishes as the intention of the evangelists. These writers, having received the tradition in spoken form, judged how it should most faithfully be kept in written language.

These 17 stories are offered as a beginning, not an end. It is my hope that when read, these retellings will prompt believers to compose in meditation and prayer, in word, song and art, in dreams and visions, their own copies of scenes from the life of Jesus. I am certain that even without this encouragement, the Holy Spirit will continue to prompt the telling of the rich and subtle meaning of the life of Jesus. This is work of the Spirit that never ends. St. John was on to this when he wrote, "There are also many other things which Jesus did; if all were written down, the world itself, I suppose, would not hold all the books that would have to be written" (Jn 21:25).

1

Angel Gabriel Visits the Priest Zechariah

Then there appeared to him the angel of the Lord, standing on the right of the altar of incense. The sight disturbed Zechariah and he was overcome with fear.

(Luke 1:11-12)

Zechariah was both a priest and a scandal, but wife Elizabeth covered it with a bold face. "Blessed be the Most High," she said. "The Most High will be gracious." When Zechariah responded with "May the Most High also be quick," she knew that he appreciated her attempt to console him.

However observant of the prescriptions of the law this husband and wife appeared to be, the truth was that wife Elizabeth was a barren woman for whom no more fruitful years were allotted. One and all reckoned this as God's judgment on a great personal sin. Now their graying hair renewed the gossip and

17

opprobrium by which they had been pursued throughout their unproductive wedlock. The rabbis taught that in such cases the individuals, if they were properly disposed, could explain the justice of the verdict which God had enacted. But most proved to be like priest Zechariah and wife Elizabeth; that is, unwilling as they crouched behind claims of innocence. On occasion, their rabbi would press them, "Confession, always fruitful for the soul, might be fruitful for the womb as well."

Being of Aaron's line, Zechariah was to travel twice during each year to Jerusalem. There he took his place among 300 other colleagues of the section of priesthood called Abijah for one week of duty in the sumptuous temple which King Herod had completed only three years before.

When Zechariah was young, that is, when his hopes for a family were bright, he had a part in the construction of the temple. He served as one of the thousand sons of Aaron whom King Herod had trained as masons to lay sacred stone upon sacred stone in the innermost precincts of the temple, sanctuaries destined for such holiness that even from their construction laity were to be kept at their distance.

Dutifully each year, Zechariah traveled to Jerusalem with his saddle bags filled with linens that he and wife Elizabeth had made from lamb's wool and on which she had embroidered designs. After selling them at the traders' stalls along the temple promenade, Zechariah would return with saddle bags filled with grains and salts needed for their pantry.

Once arrived in Jerusalem, the entire presbyterate of Abijah assembled in solemn conclave in a hall within Antonia fortress. It was proximate to the temple and spacious for their purposes, for it had barracks and lavish baths. At the doors of the hall stood the two who held the office of Scourge. Though their presence was largely symbolic now, during a previous era it had been their task to lay punishment with a stick over the backs of those who tried to gain advantage during election.

Here in this fine place the priesthood met to choose by lots the seven who were to enter the sanctuary and offer the evening sacrifice of incense through the coming week of duty. Naturally, it was the ambition of any priest to be chosen for this roster.

Years passed and the lotteries were as unwilling as wife Elizabeth's womb. Like life itself, for Zechariah, these journeys had become something to endure. As with kin in the village, among priest cousins in Jerusalem, Zechariah encountered silent accusation, initially from their eyes, but more lately through their avoidance. Frankly, on each occasion, the prospect of the lottery filled him with trepidation; for, now with wife Elizabeth's barrenness confirmed by the judgment of the years, to have the lots fall upon him would be an unspeakable scandal for the priestly name of Abijah.

But when he showed his dread about going, wife Elizabeth was resolute. Remember how she always sought to console him. "Husband, it is ordained for you to be part of the assembly of Abijah. It is ordained that you take your place in the conclave, and, if it be the will of the Most High, to stand for priestly service. My husband, since we are both of Aaron's line, our lineage is pure. We are not the sinners all suppose. The Most High will be gracious. Blessed be the Most High."

But the high priest was none too gracious about Zechariah's semiannual appearance and presided nervously over each conclave of Abijah, always relieved when consecutive throws of dice eliminated Zechariah from the company of the privileged; always relieved, that is, until the conclave when the unthinkable, alas, occurred.

This time Zechariah advanced with each scramble of the dice both to destiny and to the altar. The electors froze with apprehension as, in the final round, Zechariah emerged from the presbyterate as the first of the seven elected for service.

One of those whom the lots had not chosen was an ambitious Pharisee. Much to the man's dismay, he had never advanced. His full face and protruding waist annoyed him as well, for he practiced fasting. Complaining to the one who sat next to him, he said, "Just between you and me, this man is a sinner. His wife is barren. My wife is not barren. We have sons. The law is clear. Where are his sons? The Most High knows that my wife and I are upstanding. Surely this man is a sinner. He cannot win election. If necessary, I will appear before King Herod." He was always appearing before King Herod, it seemed.

This ambitious Pharisee had chosen his audience poorly, for the one upon whom he poured his grievance had known for years of the complaining spirit of this man and of the destruction he had accomplished in audiences with King Herod. Reacting to the sanctimonious character of his neighbor, he spoke back as if brushing away a pesky gnat. "Moses has made clear his intention," he said. "The lots must be obeyed."

And so it was. In spite of the indictment of wife Elizabeth's barrenness, in spite of the righteousness of the Pharisee who though he practiced fasting and had sons, had never advanced, in spite of Zechariah's own reluctance, the lots had chosen. As it was prescribed, this son of Aaron was to enter the sanctuary and offer evening sacrifice. Blessed be the Most High, indeed.

Zechariah rose from his place and went to the sacristy. From a cedar chest an attending Levite fitted him and the others selected with vestments of priestly office. First was a tunic made of purple wool, with wide crimson cuffs and borders. Fixed along the lower hem were small bells of gold, oblong in shape, that were speeched to ring deeply. A cumbersome train impeded, as was only right, the movement or haste that would be regarded in poor taste for the sanctuary. Over the tunic was placed the splendid ephod that hung by shoulder straps from breast to knees. On the straps were onyx stones, mounted in settings of golden net and engraved with names of the sons of Israel. Over the ephod, and no less weighty for its jewels, was placed the pectoral of judgment. In this there were four rows of stones, as it was prescribed in the law: sard, topaz, carbuncle, for the first row; emerald, sapphire, diamond, for the second; hyacinth, ruby, amethyst, for the third; and, for the fourth, beryl, onyx and jasper. Twelve in number, these too bore the names of the sons of Israel. The pectoral hung from chains of gold that had been twisted and fashioned into cords. Then for the head, there was a turban of fine linen. Fixed on the turban was a diadem of unalloyed gold. Engraved on this, Zechariah read the words, "Consecrated to the Most High."

Heavy the turban and the tunic, heavy the amethyst and

the jasper, heavy the ephod and the pectoral of judgment, heavy the engravings and the purple, heavy it all upon Zechariah's neck and arms; and, yes, upon his heart as well. He and the others appeared vested in the conclave. As he passed the bench of the self-praising Pharisee, he heard him remark contemptuously, "See the sinner now, dressed according to his office, if not according to his integrity. May the Most High not judge him for his desecration of the altar and scandal to Israel."

When the presbyterate had come to order again the dean of Abijah read from father Moses to the sacred and now vested rota the prescription regarding temple service for which they had been chosen:

> Aaron must burn fragrant incense each morning
> when he trims the lamps, and between the two
> evenings, when Aaron puts the lamps back, he must
> burn it again. You must make these offerings of
> incense before the Most High unfailingly from gener-
> ation to generation (Ex 30:7-8).

Then before Zechariah's appointed hour, another Levite reviewed with him the text and rubrics that once beyond the curtain and before the altar, it would be for Zechariah alone to enact in the name of all the people. For this priest, one fact had become clear: honor demanded his ministrations. Zechariah was profoundly moved by the responsibility that was his. Yes, it was now so obvious: personal preference, the uproar of Abijah and scandal to the faithful not withstanding; on this day, the rites of the temple were to be carried forth as it was prescribed for the generations, and carried forth by the raising of his hands, the hands of the priest Zechariah, so wholly compromised as they were by Elizabeth's barrenness.

On his day, when all was in readiness and the hour had come, he entered the holy place through the curtain. Though as a mason Zechariah had known the sacred enclosure before, now it was different. This time there was not a trowel in his hand and mortar beneath his nails. Now there was precious wear and ephod, sapphire and ruby, honor and highest of obligations. He would fulfill every rubric as worthily as he knew. Lighting coals that had been set in the brazier, he sprinkled frankincense and other aromatic resins derived from gums and spices upon them in profligate fashion. Then, grasping its long chain, he swung the brazier round and round about the altar in fulsome circles; and, as prescribed in the law, he sung in a fulsome way as well the lyrics of the psalm.

> The Most High, I am calling, hurry to me,
>> listen to me, I am invoking you.
> My prayers rise like incense,
>> my hands like the evening offering (Ps 141:1,2).

His soul added to these words composed by father David those lyrics composed by wife Elizabeth. "May the Most High be gracious!" he prayed as each arc of the censer hastened the prayer and worship of all Israel before the kingdom throne of the Most High. In this fashion did Zechariah intercede for mercy upon the household of Israel that was barren of a savior, and for mercy, too, upon the household of Zechariah and wife Elizabeth which was barren of a firstborn and thus so wholly compromised.

Then something occurred. He saw the smoke of offering collect at the right of the altar. In fact, it appeared to gather to itself and take shape and form. While remaining fluid, it seemed more substantial than smoke is allowed to be. Then strange light issued forth from within and the smoke stood still. Now it was no longer smoke, but was as definite as the shape of a person, but of a woman or a man, priest Zechariah was uncertain.

It had voice. Speaking, it comforted him. "Zechariah! Mercy for you. The anguish which you and wife Elizabeth have known is as lonely as it has been vast. I am angel Gabriel and have been sent to tell you of the graciousness of the Most High and the end of your loneliness."

Then the voice explained that prayer had been heard and barrenness was to end, for it had not been for the sake of sin, but for a higher reason.

"Wife Elizabeth shall conceive and bear a child and name him by the words of her prayer, 'The Most High shall be gracious'; for his will be a role in accord with the meaning of that name, the name John. He is to be filled not with strong beverage, but only with the strong Spirit of the Most High. O Faithful Israel!" the voice exclaimed, "the reign of the Most High is at hand."

Zechariah used his voice, "A sign!" he implored. "Of you, O Smoke, I ask and require a sign. I, a priest of Aaron's tribe, elected for this sanctuary, want a sign!"

"You require this of the Most High, priest?" said the Smoke.

"Indeed, a sign!" Zechariah insisted. Though he might have been a sinner, he was schooled in the scriptures. "Gideon sought a sign of the Most High. And first the fleece that lay through the night upon the earth was in the morning wet, while the ground was kept dry of dew; and then after the next night, the fleece proved to be dry while dew dampened all the surrounding earth (cf. Jg 6:37-40). So, not Gideon now but Zechariah requires a sign."

"Indeed, a sign!" he said again. And what a brazen priest Zechariah was showing himself to be. "Hezekiah sought a sign of the Most High. And it was so made that the shadow of Ahaz went backward ten steps, to show that Hezekiah was not to die but to live (cf. 2K 20:8-11). So, not Hezekiah now but Zechariah requires a sign."

"Silence!" demanded the vision.

"It is Gabriel who speaks! Zechariah, you have inherited much of Aaron's eloquence, but little of his faith. I came in smoke and in peace to you, priest. At the right hand of the altar, to the side of mercy not judgment, I have appeared. The Most High requires obedience of you and wife Elizabeth. I will mark you with a sign. What are the words of priestly blessing that you are to impart upon the people when you leave this station of service?"

Zechariah knew the words, as did every priest. He recited them to angel Gabriel, "The blessing is as prescribed in the law:

'May the Most High bless you and keep you.
May the Most High let his face shine on you
And be gracious to you.
May the Most High uncover his face to you
And bring you peace' " (Nb 6:24-26).

23

The angel answered, "Even as you say. This will be your sign," Gabriel said, "upon leaving, you will not be able to impart the blessing upon the faithful, nor indeed speak at all, until all that has been announced has been accomplished."

Becoming fluid again, the smoke diffused throughout the sanctuary and the vision ended. Angel Gabriel, messenger of the last times, had departed. Concluding the rites, Zechariah renewed the 12 loaves of shewbread on the offertory table and then departed the sanctuary and faced the assembled in the court.

The customary request of the faithful greeted him: "The blessing of father Moses!" the people cried. "The blessing of father Moses!" That twilight there could be no blessing, for priest Zechariah was without the function of speech.

Both the pious and the unbelieving there reacted. "See! The Most High has struck him!" they yelled and then they scurried forth in many directions. The Court of the Gentiles and its usual complement of tourists, pilgrims and traders collected immediately and contributed to the commotion. A Levite ran to summon the high priest from his supper. Now, in hindsight, it seemed that during the conclave good judgment should have overruled the lots. The Most High had now commented upon their boldness. Sinners best not stand at the altar. Lawyers from among the Sadducees would next be summoned to pronounce upon the authenticity of this worship. Indeed, they might deem that another should repeat it properly, someone of whose integrity they could be certain. Now many were regretful that they had dismissed the concerns of that righteous Pharisee.

Without his voice, Zechariah took hasty leave of the barracks where the conclave had been, and took leave of Jerusalem where first to him the plan of the Most High had been revealed. Though his beast was encumbered with saddle bags of grain and salt, his spirit was lightened with joy. He returned to his village and there to wife Elizabeth, to gather her hands to his. Soon he would know with his touch the contours of a swollen belly; and, in her eyes, to see already a child, a much wanted child, dance in glee, for even before conception he had been the subject of angel speech.

Blessed be the Most High, for judgment had been taken from against priest Zechariah and wife Elizabeth. The Most High had remembered and the injustice had been reversed. The name would be John, because wife Elizabeth had been correct all along. The Most High had been gracious, even if not quick.

Though his throat was silenced, Zechariah's soul still retained its voice and as he passed along the road, he sung in his soul lyrics of a new psalm, one that he would sing aloud after the Most High, in his good judgment, had restored wind to his lungs:

> And you, little child,
> you shall be called Prophet of the Most High,
> for you will go before the Lord
> to prepare a way for him (Lk 1:76).

Thus on that day, as prescribed for the temple, the priest Zechariah exercised priestly office at the altar, having had it fall to him first by lots, and then by duty, to enter the sanctuary of the Most High and burn incense there.

2

The Just Man Joseph Is Visited in a Dream

Joseph, son of David, do not be afraid to take Miriam home as your wife, because she has conceived what is in her by the Holy Spirit.

(Matthew 1:20)

The fathers had decided. This union would be appropriate. First, it had been Miriam's father, a miller of pearl barley named Joachim, that the father of Joseph had visited to testify concerning his son's character.

"Joachim, all Nazareth knows of my son Joseph. They remember how he went to Jerusalem to work for years during the construction of the temple of the Most High. While preparing beams for arcades and raising columns for courts, he mastered every use of wood and stone. Now he has learned of every tree in the Galilean woodlands, and from their laurel, cypress, fig and olive lumber can construct cabinets and tables of

27

beauty and of use. My Joseph will succeed and make a fitting husband and father of Israel, especially with Romans and their clamor for shelves for homes and rooms for banquets. Let him take Miriam, your daughter, in marriage."

Miriam and Joseph had not known one another. But when they met, "He is gentle," Miriam thought, "and hard working, too." Joseph regarded Miriam as quick witted. Her father would willingly accept the dowry that Joseph had to offer. Though not much, it was, at least, the 50 shekels silver that custom required. After this, from time to time, Joseph was seen visiting in the home of miller Joachim and wife Ann. At the well, villagers would be aware. "Behold, Joseph and Miriam! They will be betrothed before the next moon."

They were correct. Miriam and Joseph were soon betrothed before the blind rabbi of Nazareth. On that day, all were agreed when in notarizing the oath, the rabbi said that in Nazareth there were no two more fine than Joseph, the carpenter who had learned of wood and stone while working in the temple of the Most High, and Miriam, daughter of miller Joachim and wife Ann.

As custom demanded, during betrothal they lived apart. During this time carpenter Joseph began to build a home for them. Often, in the company of her mother, Miriam came to supervise. "Make sure that this door swings evenly on its hinge, my betrothed," she cautioned. "Anyone can build a home, only a carpenter can hang a door."

Wrapped heavily in the veils of propriety, the young woman Miriam was joyful and alert. She was a devout daughter of Moses, too. Joseph was pleased with the choice of a wife to which the fathers had agreed.

However, after some time carpenter Joseph noticed an awkwardness in the woman. For an entire month his betrothed had been quieter and unusually reserved. There could be no mistaking it. Her humor was gone. Then on one sabbath after the morning observances in the synagogue, the rabbi called for Joseph to remain after the assembly had been dismissed.

"Joseph, something is wrong," the rabbi began.

"Teacher," Joseph answered, "something is wrong indeed, but I do not know what. Instruct me, if you would."

"Joseph, though I am a blind man, I am not a fool."

"Teacher, I take you, as I always have, as one established before the Most High in wisdom and erudition. I have not lied. All I know is that something is amiss with my betrothed and I do not know what it is." Joseph was not prepared for the next words of the rabbi.

"Miriam, your betrothed, appears guilty of blameful conduct," the rabbi said. "Yes, Joseph, she is with child. It is now twice that she should have come to me for purification after the flowing of blood and has not. If she remains any longer outside your home, I will be forced to declare before Israel the sinner Miriam is and require that she pay the law's price for adultery.

"Listen to me, Joseph. I have known you all your life. Trust the judgment of this rabbi. Take her to yourself and accept the child that has been conceived by your human weakness with her."

The words of the rabbi rushed upon Joseph and dazed him. Should he protest his innocence or should he claim responsibility? He stood, asked the rabbi to pronounce over him the blessing of father Moses and then, shattered, walked into sabbath light.

He decided that he would not see Miriam for a week. This would give him seven full days to collect his thoughts and consider his choices. It was well known in Israel that often the Most High revealed his will during one's sleep.

At first it seemed to Joseph that this would be a simple choice between judgment and mercy. If he was to indict her for adultery, a jury would be elected to consider the testimony. Betrothed Miriam would be required to appear for a hearing. Nazareth was small, too small, in fact, to have a standing court of elders who could be convened to decide on such a difficult matter. A court would be appointed from a larger village, perhaps from Capernaum. But there could be no prediction of who would be nominated to serve. They could be distinguished for their wisdom and mercy; or, they could be a cruel and vengeful batch.

During the next few days Joseph imagined what was likely to occur. Once seated and having administered the proper oaths to the defendant and the witnesses, the trial would commence. Before deliberating, a ranking official from Jerusalem, present in Nazareth for these proceedings, would counsel the court, "Be deliberate in judgment, for whoever takes time in rendering judgment will be unruffled in judgment."

First Joseph would be called forward for testimony. "Are you the father of the child who is conceived?" they would inquire.

"No, no," Joseph would answer. "I am not the father of the child who is conceived. May the Most High have mercy. I am innocent of this deed." Perjury would be out of the question, for that would constitute an even greater forfeit of soul.

"Well, carpenter," another questioner would ask, "have you ever taken your betrothed unto your bed?"

"No, no," Joseph would answer. "I have never taken my betrothed unto my bed. May the Most High have mercy." Yes, perjury would be out of the question.

Then they would call upon Miriam. For her, of course, the questioning would be more painful and demanding. The judges would ask question after question of her, mounting a case that would, in good faith before Moses and this assembly of justice, either confirm innocence or fix guilt. As was the custom, their questions would be careful. They would so engineer their sentences that if she were lying her own word would snap as a trap ensnares its prey. Just one inconsistency here, even an awkward phrase there, would tangle to form one skein of lies and the work of this court would be accomplished.

The first information that the court would desire to know would be if her pregnancy were the result of rape, or, rather, if it were the result of seduction. Certainly Miriam would not be to blame if she had been raped. Seduction was a different matter, though. For the prevailing opinion among the rabbis of Israel was that a woman cooperated in seduction and this complicity made her no less guilty than her partner.

But, if it had been rape, there would be nothing further discussed. The elders would affirm her innocence before all concerned and call upon the Most High to strike the guilty one and address the injustice done to a virgin and to a betrothed.

In order first to make this important distinction, that is, the distinction between rape and seduction, the court would inquire as to where the sexual encounter had occurred. If it had been in the fields, the chances were more likely that the elders would conclude that it had been rape. But, if it had been in the city, rape was less feasible and her prospects in this trial were quite bleak. The prosecution would mount a strong case that she had cooperated in seduction.

"Tell us, woman," they would say, "why did you not let out a protest? Help would have come to rescue you. Has not the Most High given women voice for precisely this reason?"

As Joseph considered this, he admitted that acquittal was not likely. If it happened that she had been found innocent, still her reputation would remain tarnished beyond recovery. Allegation, however outlandish, had a way of sticking to one's skin in the villages around Galilee. At the well they would say, "Yes, free this time, but only on a technicality." If the verdict were guilty, this synagogue, scrupulous in its regard for the institution of the family, would call for death. There was no question about that.

A third possibility remained. If it were a hung jury, that is, if jurists could not reach a unanimous decision, then their last resort was a test provided for by the Torah called "the waters of bitterness." Though Joseph had never seen this administered in his native Nazareth, he had witnessed it while working in Jerusalem upon the temple of the Most High. It was something he cared not to recall.

First, the entire community would gather. One of priestly lineage would be needed to preside over this assembly. Naturally, men would sit in the center of the assembly, but it was also critical that young men and young women be in attendance, for it was thought that prudence could be frightened into them by what they were about to witness.

The eldest of the community would read the passage from the Torah in which the test for innocence is outlined:

> The priest shall take living water in an earthen jar,
> and on the water throw dust that he has taken from
> the floor of the tabernacle. He is then to put the
> woman on oath. He shall say to her: "If it is not true

31

that a man has slept with you, then may this water of bitterness and cursing do you no harm. But if it true that you have gone astray, while under your husband's authority, that you have disgraced yourself by sharing your bed with a man other than your husband, may the Most High make of you a curse among your people, making your thigh shrivel and your belly swell" (Nb 5:17-22).

Then the priest would make the woman drink this water of bitterness.

Would that there were more choices. If rather than calling for a trial, Joseph chose mercy and asked for a divorce, Miriam would go free, but Joseph would be known as a man not able to stand by the word which he had sworn before father Moses. Miriam would be divorced quietly and Joseph would provide her with funds until the time that she would marry, that is, if anyone would have her.

Carpenter Joseph considered these options. On the one hand, there was a formal trial with its chance of acquittal but likelihood of judgment. On the other hand, he could proceed with a quiet divorce, pay personally and abide for his lifetime the misunderstanding of others.

He decided. It would be mercy. Best not even to speak with Miriam about the decision. No need to put her through that. Whatever had occurred, Miriam had suffered enough.

No, he would not even ask her about it. He would secure the services of a Pharisee who trafficked in this messy divorce business and have him compose the writ of dismissal.

Yes, carpenter Joseph would pay the fine to the temple for failure to keep his part of the contract. The Pharisee would make that transaction and then add a percentage to the fine for his efforts. Yes, carpenter Joseph would provide Miriam funds until such a time that she could be married. With these agreements made, the Pharisee who trafficked in these unpleasantries would declare the contract null and void. Perhaps someone then would blow a horn. Each would again be free to marry. Yes, it was the best solution, even if it was costly.

Other reasons than the dedicating of funds made it costly. It would appear that Joseph was accepting blame for a situation for which he was not responsible. Joseph could deal with those appearances. What was more costly than the funds and more difficult than dealing with appearances would be the pain his beloved Miriam might experience if she reasoned that he had not accepted her word of innocence. Joseph wished there was a way he could demonstrate his confidence in her integrity. In his heart, there was no question of it, for he gave her every benefit of the doubt. Wisdom now demanded action before the village and before the law. Action was urgent and in her best interest, even if it was costly to his purse, to his pride and most costly to his tender love.

Joseph defended by the law now knew that from that same law Miriam needed to be protected. He could not be frozen in considerations of justice, selfish or generous however these might be. Whether Miriam was innocent or guilty, Joseph's action would be a mercy for his betrothed who had either made a mistake and shown weakness, or who had been the victim of cruel violence. Joseph was satisfied that he had done the best he could.

Thus that sabbath did carpenter Joseph arrive at his decision to divorce quietly his betrothed Miriam who was with child. It was on the same sabbath after the sun had set, the sabbath on which the blind rabbi had been the one to explain the news, the awful, incomprehensible news. Joseph slept with the peaceful sleep of the merciful and with the relief of those who have decided.

During the next four nights, carpenter Joseph, having decided upon mercy and not on judgment, was visited by the Most High in his dreams. Four times through this week he was touched mightily in his sleep and awoke puzzling the meaning of visions that he had been given.

In the first of these dreams, Tamar, widow of Er, the first-born of Judah, appeared to carpenter Joseph. In this vision, Tamar was giving birth to the twins Perez and Zerah (cf. Gn 38:30).

Her own husband had died leaving her childless and her brothers-in-law had failed, too, in their responsibility to conceive a son in the name of their deceased brother. On the foot of the bed was prostitute's clothing. Tamar had worn this to deceive her father-in-law Judah into having the intercourse with her which was both his duty and her right.

As the vision continued, dreamer Joseph saw his betrothed serving as midwife for Tamar. The dreamer saw Miriam, upon realizing that it was to be a multiple birth, tie scarlet thread to the hand of Zerah as it emerged in order to secure for him the all important identification as first-born.

In the morning, dreamer Joseph went to the rabbi and asked for an interpretation of the dream in which Tamar had appeared. The rabbi asked Joseph to take the scroll of scripture in which the story of Tamar was recorded for the sons and daughters of Israel and to read it carefully to him.

After hearing it read and thinking for some time about the word of scripture, the rabbi said to Joseph, "Widow Tamar, Joseph, was a woman of determination and justice; a willing agent, over and against all suspicious appearances, of the plan of the Most High.

"You ask me what it can mean, Joseph. The Most High triumphs over all human obstacles, even the great obstacle, that of appearances. Can what first scandalizes the suspicious eye be in the end the channel by which the Most High chooses to cut short the time?"

The second night prostitute Rahab of Jericho and betrothed Miriam appeared to carpenter Joseph. In this vision, dreamer Joseph entered Rahab's house which was full of family, friends and acquaintances. By shrewd, prior negotiations, Rahab had guaranteed the protection of all these during Israel's siege of Jericho. From the window of the house was draped the scarlet cloth that signaled the advancing Israelites that this was the household that they had agreed to spare. Within the walls of this house, in the midst of this mob of gentiles of Jericho, and sharing in the protection that Rahab had secured from the scouts of the Israelites, was Miriam. Then the dreamer heard gentile Rahab say to Miriam: "The Most High your Lord is God both in heaven above and on earth beneath" (Jos 2:11).

When morning came, dreamer Joseph sought the rabbi, explained the dream and asked for an interpretation of it. Again, Joseph was told to open the scroll in which the story of Rahab was recorded and to read it to the rabbi.

He said to Joseph, "Prostitute Rahab, Joseph, was saved by faith and justified by deeds on behalf of her family; a willing agent, in spite of her status as a gentile and a woman, of the plan of the Most High.

"You ask me what it means. The Most High triumphs over all human obstacles. Even what appears to the suspicious eye as weak, can be the channel by which the Most High acts."

The third night, Joseph dreamed again. Now Moabite Ruth and her mother-in-law Naomi appeared. In this vision, Joseph's betrothed, Miriam, walked in the company of widows Ruth and Naomi. The dreamer understood that while Orpah, sister-in-law to Ruth and also a widow, had departed company to return to her own people, Ruth had decided to proceed with her mother-in-law to a land wherein she would always be regarded as a foreigner. The dreamer heard Ruth, against her mother-in-law's own counsel, insist to Naomi and to Miriam:

> Wherever you go, I will go,
> Wherever you live, I will live.
> Your people shall be my people,
> and your God, my God (Rt 1:16).

Again, with the light of morning, dreamer Joseph went to the rabbi. Again the scroll came down. And, again as Joseph read the word of scripture, the rabbi considered the story and pondered the meaning of Joseph's dream.

The rabbi said, "Gentile Ruth, Joseph, left home and family in devotion to her mother-in-law; in her profound openness, a willing agent of God's plan. The Most High triumphs over all human obstacles.

"You ask me what it means. Even what appears to the suspicious eye as foolishness can be the channel by which the Most High chooses to intervene."

On the fourth and final night of dreams, David and his wife Bathsheba, the widow of Uriah the Hittite, appeared to dreamer Joseph. Their firstborn, having been conceived during their adultery, had just died. The dreamer understood that David had ended his week-long vigil of prayer, fasting and sackcloth by which he had observed the time of the child's illness. The dreamer saw King David wash and anoint himself and return to the side of his wife.

35

With Bathsheba was Miriam who announced to David and his wife that their sin had been forgiven and that they would conceive again and now give birth to a child destined for wisdom in Israel. They would name the child Solomon. Having first comforted Bathsheba and David on their loss, now the betrothed rejoiced with them over glad news.

For the final time, dreamer Joseph went to the rabbi and asked for an interpretation of the dream. As on the other mornings, on this one, too, after the scroll had been read, the rabbi spoke, "Adulteress Bathsheba, Joseph, first lost her husband to David's sin and then a child to God's anger, but still was worthy of the plan of the Most High; a willing agent, not disqualified by her sinful humanity from sharing in the plan of the Most High."

This time it was Joseph who suggested the meaning of the dream to the rabbi. "The Most High triumphs over all human obstacles. Even what appears to the suspicious eye as the unworthiness of the sinner can be the channel by which the Most High chooses to intervene."

The rabbi approved. "Joseph, you have dreamed mightily this week. Only the Spirit within you can fathom the deepest meaning of these visions. Let me suggest that perhaps Miriam, like these faithful women of Israel of whom you have dreamed, has been destined, too, to be instrument of the Most High, in spite of human appearances. Joseph, your Miriam is blessed among the women of Israel; and blessed, too, the fruit of her womb."

Joseph again pondered the meaning of these dreams in which his betrothed appeared with gentile women. He realized that Miriam had been called to stand with these great women of Israel's history.

Joseph hurried to Miriam and admitted that he had known that she was with child. Then this young woman, not yet 13, explained to beloved Joseph the unexplainable story of a pregnancy whose origin was not of the human spirit but of God's Spirit and of the one for whose coming both had prayed on their parents' knees.

"Joseph," she announced confidently, "it is now to be accomplished among us."

"Blessed be the Most High," dreamer Joseph answered, "he shows forth his plan in visions and cuts short the time."

He told her of his four nights of dreams. Though both made plans to live together immediately, the rabbi recommended that it would be prudential if instead she spent time away from the village, for already mean words had been spoken, and the townsfolk of Nazareth seemed anxious to believe the worst.

Then remarkable word arrived that a cousin of Miriam, Elizabeth by name, had conceived. It had been a springtime of the remarkable. Being barren, this woman of Aaron's line had lived a long life during which she was required to abide the mean words of judgment. But now, though advanced beyond the usual years of childbearing, in fact, far beyond them, she was heavy with child. To her home Miriam could hasten and remain there for the duration of Elizabeth's confinement. There in the home of Zechariah and Elizabeth, Miriam could have privacy. Before Miriam set off to visit kin in another village, she directed final words of instruction to Joseph about the dwelling he would continue to construct in her absence. Upon her return the rabbi would perform the wedding ceremony. It would be done discretely. Their marriage would begin and the child would be welcomed, for this was a child whose importance to the people of Israel had been explained in dreams and visions.

After her departure, Joseph returned to the synagogue. He entered the library in which the scrolls of law and prophets were kept on shelves behind heavy curtains. He opened the scroll of Isaiah and read the prophet's mysterious verse: "A virgin shall conceive and bear a child."

Then he recalled Miriam's confidence, "Joseph, it is now to be accomplished among us."

3

Census and Birth

So Joseph set out from the town of Nazareth in Galilee and traveled up to Judea, to the town of David called Bethlehem, since he was of David's House and line, in order to be registered together with Miriam, his betrothed, who was with child. While they were there the time came for her to have her child, and she gave birth to a son, her firstborn.

(Luke 2:4-6)

They had traveled the 90 miles in the safe escort of a caravan. For this trip they made their progress on beasts. Ordinarily, it would have been more pious, more devout and edifying for them to have traveled on foot, but, this was no pilgrimage of devotion. This journey was not for one of the feasts of the Most High. Instead, this was an obligation, a hated one, but one, nevertheless, to be acquitted. The caravan had been a smart move. For each night when they stopped along their route they heard more stories of assault on the roadways which connected northern villages of Galilee to southern ones of Judea, like Bethlehem, near Jerusalem. As if Rome itself were not an adversary great enough against which a nation ought to be united, these people practiced assault one against the other.

It troubled Miriam how husband Joseph could be cynical. "This census will be as good for robbers as it will for Caesar," he complained. One cousin tried to raise his spirit by quoting the law, "Joseph, it is written, 'You shall hear the great and the small alike' " (Dt 1:17). But even against this, Joseph answered: "It is also written, 'Let all of Israel love work and hate lordship.' "

The feast of Dedication was at hand. When they made camp on high ground overlooking a village they could see the bonfires the people had lit for observance of the feast. Approaching Jerusalem, they saw the greatest of the fires. On streets and alleys, in fields and squares and on stone rooftops, bonfires were to be seen. So impressive were the blazes that it was commonly remarked that if you had never seen the feast, you would not know what joy was. You simply could not understand the meaning of joy. For this feast commemorated purification of the temple. But neither the bonfires nor the tradition of joy were of much consolation to Joseph. If somewhere during these nights there was joy, Joseph was beyond its power.

Though Bethlehem was husband Joseph's ancestral city, he had only seen its twin hills a few times before, and then only for reasons of employment. On occasion he had heard there was work for him there. For example, once walls needed to be added to enlarge a synagogue, and, at other times tables were to be built for new homes that the rich had designed.

The reason for this trip and for this caravan marked by neither prayerful gladness nor the Holy Spirit was different. Now Caesar's legions needed to be fed. So heads were to be counted for a tax. Herod was desirous of presenting the high numbers that make an impression on an emperor. Joseph tried to be resigned. No use losing soul over this, he decided. Perhaps, in his providence, the Most High would draw some good from this, Joseph hoped. In any case, what was to be done but for this son of David to travel on to David's city, there to have the counting over with and the impression made? And as an added burden, wife Miriam, the one who did not find his cynicism agreeable, was pregnant, and due to deliver in a week or two. For her this passage would be arduous and she would be sorely tired by the end of it.

After arrival in father David's city, they searched for somewhere to provide for the beasts that had served them so well and a place to provide for their own bones which had also served them. The limestone cave had been the right choice.

Ordinarily the inn was fine for travelers. Proximate both to the bazaars and the well, it also provided one with the company and fires of fellow travelers. There was no place for wife Miriam and carpenter Joseph in the inn, for she was sleeping poorly. When all was said and done, at best, inns were paddocks where mule or ass could be tethered and fed. Next to the posts and troughs travelers bedded down for sleep. No, Bethlehem's inn was not the place for a daughter of Israel, gone as far as she with child, to rest. Joseph was sure of this. For there would be no relief from the activity and smell of the place. Husband Joseph would not require wife Miriam to accommodate herself to this. So, as soon as they arrived he went to the bazaar to purchase grain and onions and to discover if other accommodations, appropriate to their circumstances, were available.

One of his kin suggested he see a man whose right arm was withered and speech slurred, but who had many connections. At first, the man listened with perfect indifference to Joseph's story. But when he felt a half-shekel pressed into his good palm, his disposition became more agreeable.

"Yes," he said. "I can direct you to a cave that will suit your needs. Nearby, there is a flock whose shepherds are waiting for shearing to begin. Young shepherds, always good for fresh figs and always pleased for a fresh chance to steal, welcome visitors. This time of year they are bored and are anxious to fleece. You will be quite welcome," he said wryly.

The cave was suitable and once arrived, husband Joseph seemed relieved. "Blessed be the Most High," he said, "he shelters the homeless." Wife Miriam was pleased with the improvement in her husband's spirit.

41

As long as the rains held off, the animals could remain outside, leaving the interior of the cave for them. At the mouth of the cave was a spacious clearance. Once settled, Joseph laid out a bed of straw inside upon which the two could sleep. From a woolen bag, he took a flint rock and made fire. Then, from the same saddle bag, wife Miriam produced the menorah, the candelabrum that husband Joseph had carved from aromatic cedar long ago during his Jerusalem days. They lit three of its lamps, for it was the third night of the feast of Dedication.

The next morning, when shepherds made their first visit, the husband and wife were ready for them. For before leaving Nazareth husband Joseph had chiseled figurines from ebony wood that he intended to sell in Bethlehem. Now, instead, he presented them as gifts to the shepherds. Wife Miriam, who had woven woolen caps and on them embroidered symbols of the tribes of Israel, presented these as well. Never in all Israel was wood and wool better spent, for these handsome figurines and handsome caps won over the shepherds.

Soon the shepherds were wearing their new woolen caps and filling skins with water and goat's milk for the couple and bringing them pieces of lamb's wool. At the time, little did Miriam expect that these would serve as swaddling for her infant. However reduced their conditions were and however undesirable it was to be away from family and relations during this time, husband Joseph and wife Miriam had transformed this cave and its clearance on the outskirts of father David's city Bethlehem into a suitable dwelling and a habitation of joy for Israel. And, no small triumph, they had made neighbors of the shepherds.

However, on the streets of father David's city Bethlehem, there was no joy for Israel. The streets of all Judean cities were hot with fire against this census and the tax and military conscription it augured. Father David's city proved no exception. The obligation that Joseph had hoped would be acquitted in one day or two had now demanded more than a week of his patience. Descendants of father David's harem, filled the narrow streets of Bethlehem throughout the day with furious anger. One of the kin expressed it in this way, "They tax our produce and our lands. They tax our animals and our occupations. When Caesar has a birthday or a triumph, we are rewarded with a tax. Even our women are taxed fourfold to ride a beast along his pavements. Fine pavements they are."

So deep and unrelenting was the hostility that the soldiers whose task it was to make the census inscriptions could not organize the men into lines even to begin their count. If King Herod were informed of the unrest here, he would call for the shedding of blood on the stones of father David's city and upon the descendants of father David's harem, for Herod brooked no disregard for his desires. Husband Joseph returned to wife Miriam at twilight of each day and with disappointment reported to her the slow progress of the census and the abiding rage that they, in their cave —blessed be the Most High for every comfort, no matter how small—had been spared.

The days of Dedication and the days of unrest continued. On the final day of the feast Joseph returned somewhat later than his usual time and discovered that Miriam had not waited for his arrival to light the final branch of the menorah.

"Husband Joseph," she announced, "tonight there will be one more head in father David's city for Caesar to count." The days of her confinement had come to their end. Labor had begun. While wife Miriam insisted she was ready to be delivered of the child, husband Joseph insisted that she was not.

"Are you sure?" he asked, as he counted reluctantly to nine on his fingers, wishing he could argue with the arithmetic. "I am sure," she said. Then he argued, "I am a carpenter and not a midwife."

This is one argument that no husband has ever won. On this wife Miriam would have the final word. Now it was her turn for pronouncement.

"Husband," she said, "we will see what you are by the time morning light falls upon this cave from the east."

But she could not tease him more. Labor was intense and frequent now. There was not even time for Joseph to fetch a midwife from town.

Husband Joseph did his best. "You need to concentrate," he counseled her. He was nervous. "I will recite the Torah," he said, "while you do what you need to do." He was very nervous and unsure of what was needed. Though his mother had borne many children, whenever time had come for her to deliver, he had been directed to the woods to look for lumber suitable for a crib. The fact that they already had a crib did not seem to matter. Now Joseph thought, "Why once did I not stay at my mother's side to learn?" When nervous like this, he amused his wife beyond all expression.

The recitation began: "In the beginning God created the heavens and the earth. Now the earth was a formless void, there was darkness over the deep, and God's spirit hovered over the water . . ."

The labor of mother Miriam was swift. She had been right on both counts. First, Caesar would have one more head to count; and, also, that night they would see what her husband was. For, to his own surprise, midwife Joseph did all that was required.

By the flickering branch lights of a menorah; while at the mouth of their cave shepherds gathered to wring their hands, to condemn the Caesar and the census that had occasioned such hardship, and to carry and then make hot the water for washings; while nervous, very nervous, Joseph recited the story of creation and wiped his wife's brow; that night a child was born in the city of Bethlehem. One more descendant from the harem of David, great king of Israel, was born.

Mother Miriam heard the newborn cry as the air of earth filled for the first time the lungs of God. As husband Joseph washed the child, she watched. But she was so tired. Gathering her strength, she spoke to husband Joseph, "You must be the first to call him by the name the angel gave."

Then Joseph held the crying child, vulnerable and poor against his calloused hands. "Be still, Jesus," he said, "your mother and I are here." Then with all of a father's love, he kissed this son upon the head.

Joseph now employed the swaddling. Supervisory direction from mother Miriam was forthcoming. There was more crying and with good cause. "Not so tightly, my husband," Miriam protested. Finally, she assumed the operation. Then as the newborn, all properly bound and constricted, was placed against the mother's breast for his first taste of nourishment, the carpenter sang, in great joy, the psalm:

> The Most High's oracle to you, my Lord, "Sit at my
>   right hand
> and I will make your enemies a footstool for you."

> Royal dignity was yours from the day you were born,
>   on the holy mountains,
> royal from the womb, from the dawn of your earliest
>   days (Ps 110:1,3).

Mother Miriam nodded in approval at the psalm, and child Jesus was made content by the feeding. Again she entrusted the infant to husband Joseph. Then came the burp, none too solemn a sound, but glorious enough in its own right. "Blessed be the Most High," listener Joseph said, "for every sound that ascends to heaven." This was one blessing that night that wife Miriam could not hear, for she had drifted away. Sleep had come to her at last, and with it, peace.

Early next morning, Joseph traveled into town where he would try to excuse himself from the census proceedings. There news of the birth of a first-born son had preceded him and spread rapidly among visitors to the city. Joseph willingly provided commentary. "Yes, wife Miriam was nervous and frightened, but she relied on my strength and knowledge."

Then returning, mother Miriam asked husband Joseph to take the infant outside to see the sun and be seen by the shepherds who had stayed throughout the night and were joyful beyond description. One by one he allowed them to approach and softly touch the child and the swaddling.

"So small," exclaimed one of them, as if trying to decide if something as tender and amazing as this could be real.

The infant by then had assumed a healthy shade of pink and had become warm in his strips of wool. Ebony creatures which carpenter Joseph had first offered as tokens of alliance were now, in return, given by shepherd hands as the infant's first possessions, becoming tokens now of an altogether new alliance of mercy and friendship.

Moved by the sight of this new infant's life, one shepherd, not much accustomed to composing praise, exclaimed, "Glory to the Most High!" Another said, "Peace on earth to all of good will."

Thus it was that in a city far from Nazareth in Galilee, did the confinement of Miriam end, a confinement first announced to her in the dream during which she had been visited by angel Gabriel. At her side that night was husband Joseph; and, sharing in these joys as well, were shepherds, who, by the sight of this birth were made anxious both for praise and for peace.

4

The Lost Sheep

"What man among you with a hundred sheep, losing one, would not leave the ninety-nine in the wilderness and go after the missing one till he found it?"

(Luke 15:4)

Father Joseph conferred slingshot and crook upon the son as if he were investing the high priest with insignia of office. "If you are to be a good shepherd," he said as he presented the sling, "you will need this to fend off jackals and thieves." While the forked slingshot had been hewn by the father from a block of hard oak, the walking cane needed to be of common wood. Its extended length made lightness essential. Sycamore was chosen. In fact, so extended in length was it that it dwarfed the son by two feet when he stood with it. Father Joseph showed him how to adjust its curl properly. "It points outward," he said.

Since sheep were such a mischievous bunch, a shepherd needed a long crook so that from a distance he could poke one into obedience or perhaps even rescue a wayward member of the assem-

47

bly from wandering into harm's way. The father had so sanded the crook that it had a perfectly smooth finish. He said, "A slingshot and crook worthy of our father David, who was also a shepherd."

Remembering the fate of Abel, another shepherd, Mother Miriam was less sanguine. She observed this scene with displeasure, neither impressed by these insignia nor amused by the thought of the jackals and thieves against whom they guarded. The son was aware.

"Woman, both by Moses and the law, I am a man," he said. He was over 12 years.

"My son," answered the mother, "you are but 15 with a face as smooth as that crook. You must learn what every son of Israel learns: mothers know of matters of which the law in all its greatness is ignorant."

She was resigned, though, for these two men had already decided and protest of hers was not to prevail. In fact, theirs was little choice. A new tax collector, anxious to impress the governor by large revenue, reached ever more deeply into the pockets of the townspeople of Nazareth. Now husband Joseph was a full year in arrears of payments. On any day the collector could come to confiscate his tools. Without hammer and square, saw and plane, this family would go hungry. It was necessary for Jesus, at 15 and beardless, to hire himself for shepherd's work.

It happened that during each winter, a certain owner would lead a flock into their area of Galilee, to take advantage of the long grass occasioned by winter rains. There his sheep and goats would stay until the spring lambing and shearing were complete. They would drink daily of the water that collected in the craters of Nazareth rocks.

The coming of the herd was a relief for the overtaxed economy of this village, for once the men had completed the shearing, wool would be washed, combed and spun by Nazareth women. Then it was bundled by their men and carried off for sale at either local lake town bazaars, or transported to the south, where it was traded in stalls along the great temple colonnade.

At their synagogue was a blind rabbi who had taken

interest in Joseph and Miriam since the time of their engagement. Jesus, too, he loved. To the synagogue many times each week Jesus would go and help the blind rabbi. Jesus often read to the rabbi from scrolls on which the law and the prophets were written. At times the rabbi feared that he allowed Jesus to read at too much length to him; but, when asked if he had read enough for the day, Jesus would answer, "The more Torah, the more life." He would help the rabbi provide for visitors to town that were offered the hospitality of the synagogue; and, on sabbath, through the eyes and voice of Jesus, the rabbi would lead the assembly through the services.

Understanding the reduced means of Joseph and Miriam, the blind rabbi showed great kindness. He prevailed upon the owner of the herd to hire young Jesus. Agreeing, the owner said that if Jesus were employed, it would be for the night watch, for that was when the services of another shepherd were needed. Jesus, at 15 and still without whiskers, did not mind. The one who cared for the flock at night was a shepherd named Jesse. The owner explained to Jesus that he would be working with an experienced shepherd, some ten years older. "Jesse will be good for you," the owner said. Jesus answered, "Jesse is going to like me."

Jesse was something of a veteran at all this. He followed the herd from place to place for the owner; and, by the time Jesus came to meet him, had tended it for four years. It was only when the herd came to chew the winter grass of Galilee and when the ewes were about to lamb, that he really was in need of extra help. When the owner told him that he had hired a local teenager who was in need of help, he was pleased.

So it was that late each afternoon, Jesus would go into the hills to meet the herd at the place where it had taken water that day. Attached to his shepherd's girdle was a sack, in which he carried the bread, cheese, olives and raisins that would sustain him until the dawn. There was a skin, too, for wine or water. Given the cold Galilee nights, wine was warmer for the soul than water. Once with the flock, goat's milk, of course, could always be had.

Upon arrival, he and Jesse first counted and then took

possession of the hundred lambs and goats from the shepherds who tended the flock by day. While the less experienced
Jesus counted, the veteran Jesse, expert with his hands and
expert with the curl of his crook, detained each sheep for
examination. With his free hand he checked the fleece for
pustules or carbuncles that indicated a diseased animal. Since
anthrax is highly contagious, any infected animal would have
to be destroyed immediately. To date, winter had been kind.
Thus far there had not been ominous signs of epidemic. Goats
were less worry. In fact, by comparison to sheep, they were a
pleasure. They took their place at the head of the herd and
followed orders. Goats were resistant to disease, generous with
milk and able to descend heights without dizziness. They
enjoyed grace that their apparent awkwardness concealed.

At first it was with jealousy that Jesus observed how
the herd maintained its loyalty to Jesse's voice. Noticing his
frustration, Jesse suggested, "If you keep talking to them, soon
they will learn your voice. When I began, I recited entire
passages of the law to them. These are the only sheep in all of
Israel who can shame a scribe with their knowledge of
Moses!"

Jesus did as Jesse recommended. As the nights and weeks
of that winter in Galilee hurried along, the flock learned. Jesse
stood amazed at the ability of this very junior colleague,
especially liking how Jesus assigned nicknames. He could also
mimic those who had idiosyncrasies. "Look," Jesus would say,
"this is how 'Long Ears' runs"; or "This is 'White Back' nudg-
ing 'Fat Tail' away from the water"; or, "See, now I'm 'Curly'
being proud."

Slowly the voice of Jesus became recognized. Sheep began
to come when he called and to follow where he led. Some
responded to their nicknames. For one, there was "Cow Eyes"
who was often to be found loitering behind an old fence in the
field. When Jesus called out "Cow Eyes!" behold, from behind
the fence, an unathletic, six-horned ram, nicked in one ear but
in possession of commanding black and liquid eyes, would
come forth. An impressed shepherd Jesse said, "You are the
finest nighttime helper ever hired."

Jesus told father Joseph, "Jesse likes me. I am doing well.

Jesse likes me." But mother Miriam kept her reservations.

Though during the day the climate was temperate, as soon as the sun was no longer in the sky, warmth and kindness left the earth. Evenings and nights were cold. Having selected a spot on high ground that would provide necessary vantage over their charges, each night Jesse and Jesus built a fire to draw some of the weather and fear from the night air. The crackling sound of the blaze punctuated the narrations of the lives that they shared. It was at the fireside, when work was done, that Jesus not only imitated the idiosyncrasies of sheep, but that he also imitated those of friends and relations with wonderful accuracy.

There was, for example, neighbor Esther, who was always quoting proverbs. "When her children complain about their constant table of vegetables," Jesus said, "all she does is answer, 'The more meat, the more flies.' " Then Jesus added, "She has a remark for every situation. 'If it's not one dog barking, it's another,' is something else she often says, especially when people indulge in criticism."

Then there was Uncle Jacob, a thrifty soul who had been raised in the mountains. Though he pretended to think the worst of everyone, Jacob would drop everything to help any need. Jesus had him down, too. "People today will steal you blind," was his all-purpose review and admonition.

The parade that included the aphoristic and the cheap, and many others, too, passed before a much-delighted Jesse as mimic Jesus made these and their foibles alive under night's canopy of stars. "You are a tormentor and someone to be reckoned with one day," Jesse said, as he began to rein in his own eccentricities, fearing that he too would soon be included in the repertoire. The worst he had to suffer was when Jesus began to call him "Nighttime Jesse."

Whenever hungry these two shepherds ate cheese and drank milk or wine. The owner had been right: in spite of Jesse's casual way, Jesus was aware that Jesse was a good shepherd from whom much would be learned, for Jesse had such powers of concentration. Nighttime Jesse's attention could not be distracted, not by darkness or cold of night, not by the roar of fire or the delight of the mimicking. With one ear shepherd Jesse always listened for the flock. Discriminating among the noises of the night, Jesse was vigilant for the plaintive cry of a jackal, the haughty laugh of a hyena, or for the stealthy steps of an intruder, who might be desirous of a fine new wool sack or of lamb supper.

In the winter it rained; and rain, of course, was hardship for shepherds. From a sharp and driving rain, it was first important to protect the flock. Jesse would lead them to one of the many caves of Galilee for shelter. Jesus, who had played in these fields, knew its places better than did Jesse.

With the herd protected, a small booth could then be raised for the shepherds' protection. The junior of the two was in charge of preparing the four posts; after all, Jesse claimed, Jesus was a carpenter. As Jesus went to find four trunks of approximately the same height, he carried the wood upon his shoulders as Jesse prepared a daub roof of leaves and branches.

They acquired a pet, too, whose presence relieved routine. On arriving one evening, Jesus noticed that the chick of a falcon had fallen from its nest and been abandoned by its parents. Though as a chick it seemed innocent, the shepherds envisioned the life it would eventually lead. One day this would be the falcon that commanded, in imperious fashion, the skies over the fields of Galilee and along the coast of Gennesareth. Though born to be a predator, now it was only a few weeks old and needed help to survive. Jesus, quite solicitous for it, endlessly collected beetles and worms to satisfy its voracious appetite.

Ordinarily quite meek, the chick displayed its true inheritance while it ate. When given a worm, it speared it down with one talon while tearing at it with its sharp beak, making an end of it in short time. Jesus would often have it perch on his shoulder while he cared for the flock; or, when he was sitting by the fire, he would have it preside from the index finger of his large, dark hands. Jesse once commented that these hands seemed almost too large and dark to belong to Jesus. It almost seemed, he said to another once, that they were destined to be filled one day with some great task. Though soon the falcon flew and hunted, it returned each evening. Now that it was more mature, Jesus needed to wrap a swatch of lamb's pelt around his hand for protection from the sharpness of the talons.

For the most part, though, it was a lonely and stark life in the fields by night for shepherds. At dawn other shepherds came to relieve those faithful through the night. Inventory needed to be taken again, as well as precautions against contagion. Then Jesus and Jesse returned to their homes for the daytime sleep that, for their long and careful vigil, they now deserved.

After one rainy night watch, the count of the flock did not match. One was missing. Faster than Jesse, it was Jesus who said, "It's Cow Eyes. Cow Eyes is lost."

There was hilly terrain along the western edge of the pasture with clumps of fresh grass. Perhaps the sight of it had enticed the ram. Having climbed to high and rocky terrain, he might have become too frightened to negotiate the return passage. Leaving the flock, the shepherds took off together, across the rain-soaked pastures to the place where they hoped a frightened Cow Eyes might be.

As they climbed the hillside they could hear each other's breath become more labored. Then, in a distance, they both saw and were seen by Cow Eyes. The sight of Jesse and Jesus, and his own perilous predicament, frightened the nervous ram and it fled. The shepherds raced, too, moving swiftly across rocks and through puddles, and striding across the streams that already coursed with the year's heavy winter rain, trying in every moment not to lose sight of the ram.

Then, in the chase, Cow Eyes made one sharp and ill-considered turn into a thicket of briars and came to an abrupt halt. Thorns impaled it. Jesus, arriving first, took the crook and reached into the briars for the ram. Its reach fell short. Before the more experienced Jesse could arrive and stop him, Jesus inched further into the thicket itself, and with every additional step felt thorns tear away at the flesh on his legs. Finally, tottering over in one final grand effort for the ram, Jesus slipped on the wetness and fell headlong into the briars. By now Jesse had arrived and helped him stand. He urged strategy on his very junior colleague.

"All you had to do is speak to it," he said. "Remember, it knows your voice."

No, Jesus had not thought. Now he spoke to the ram. "Cow Eyes," he said, "come here. The others are waiting."

The ram, who knew both its name and its shepherd, moved out of the thicket and came to shepherd Jesus. While Jesus held the young ram tightly, Jesse tied together its front and rear hooves with leather bands and then hoisted Cow Eyes onto the shoulders of this younger but now proven colleague.

The two shepherds made their return over the rocks, with much rejoicing. "Blessed be the Most High," Nighttime Jesse said, "he seeks out the lost and forsaken." Once back, they returned the delinquent ram again to the rest who had waited untended for the hundredth to be restored to their assembly.

Jesse, concerned about the scratches Jesus had sustained in the thicket, returned with him that morning to the house of father Joseph and mother Miriam. The young shepherd was marked with deep abrasions and his face was beginning to swell. Briars had dug themselves into his forehead. Ticks, too, had embedded themselves across the legs and chest.

Positioning himself on a hammock, Jesus endured surgery as Jesse extracted each briar with two thin metal spikes that he managed as deftly as an emperor from the east would food sticks. As his effort on each was completed, mother Miriam who had kept her doubts, wiped the wounds with a cloth soaked in wine while Jesse anointed his face with oil. "Just like a shepherd treats the face of a sheep when it has been bitten by a snake," he said.

Then on to the ticks. In the fire, Jesse heated one long thin stick which Joseph provided. When its tip was glowing red but not yet afire, he applied it to each insect. Only intense and focused heat like this could drive a tick to release its pernicious grasp.

Over the house the falcon hovered for a moment. Then, apparently content that there was no reason for concern, soared off in search of breakfast.

In the house Jesse spoke to the patient. "You know, of course, that all you had to do was talk to the ram." Then he relented, thinking not only of how Cow Eyes had been saved, but also of the falcon, the nicknames, the many kindnesses to the blind rabbi, and of the mighty inheritance that he had seen demonstrated in the night by this young man whose dark and interesting hands, remember, seemed large enough to hold one day a great task. He said, "You have a soft heart for the flock, shepherd Jesus. You are a good shepherd."

"For the flock only? You forget the falcon?" remarked Jesus, whose sense of humor seemed to be returning after surgery.

Nighttime Jesse agreed to praise him again and said, "You are the good falconer, too." They both laughed for a moment. Then, serious again, Jesse touched the skin of Jesus once more with the business end of the burning spear and another tick unburrowed its head and fell lifeless to the earth.

5

The Good Samaritan

"Look after him," he said, "and on my way back I will make good any extra expense you might have."

(Luke 10:35)

"It will be for less than a year," he said to reassure concerned mother Miriam and father Joseph. Though neither parent was wholly sanguine concerning the plan of son Jesus to go up to Jerusalem for employment, they were wholly resigned. He was 16 and time had arrived for him to consider marriage. They were poor and could not provide the necessary dowry or *mohar*, the 50 shekels that were required both by honor and by father Moses for marriage in Israel. Understanding their conditions, the son would not burden them.

"If work is plentiful," Jesus promised, "I will return sooner than Passover with enough in my belt for a dowry and some left for you."

Though they made every effort to respond hopefully to this, they were not successful. Theirs was poor hope; for, like friends and relations, they too were dejected. It was the dark cloud of tax which never dissipated that shrouded this whole people with apathy and discouraged them from seeking the improvements that a carpenter like father Joseph could provide.

It would be foolish for Jesus to linger in these home parts. At best, he would be idle; and, at worst, like many his age, he would align himself with Zealots, headstrong fomenters of rebellion against imperial supremacy. Fathers, like Joseph, had seen more than sons. They complained that this was an improbable cause if ever there was one. While Caesar equipped his artillery with ballistics that weighed 770 pounds, against these the Zealots would rush with stones and anger. Honestly, fathers commented, had these boys received the spirit of father David? Did they believe that David's carnage of Goliath was likely to occur in Galilee?

Through the years of adolescence Jesus had been an apprentice to father Joseph and had learned the diverse trade of carpentry. While his talent was not as developed as father Joseph's, he was trained enough to be of worth in Jerusalem. Agreed, he was hopeful; but it was with good reason. Friends of mother Miriam and carpenter Joseph had assured them that it would be wise at this time to allow son Jesus to leave Nazareth and go up to Jerusalem. Friends returning to Nazareth from the city of the Most High suggested that however unpolished were the skills of this young carpenter, in Jerusalem work could be found. "If there are funds and lumber enough," they reasoned, "and if Herod has not lost determination that this shrine to honor the Most High and affirm his own tarnished name among our nation be built, there will be work for young Jesus to earn more than the silver needed for his dowry." So, it would be to Jerusalem that Jesus would go to contribute, as had father Joseph when he was young and in need of silver for a dowry bag, to the construction of the temple of the Most High.

The foreman who had supervised the services of father Joseph still served in the temple yards. Upon arrival, Jesus would locate this man. Surely the man would recognize the name of carpenter Joseph from Nazareth and recall how satisfied all had been with his services long ago. "Blessed be the Most High who makes the years to pass swiftly," he would exclaim, "this is the son, already apprenticed with stone and lumber, and already in need of silver to fill a dowry bag for a bride."

So it was that at 16 years, son Jesus, having served as apprentice to his father, went to Jerusalem, there to present himself to the foreman.

Yes, of course, the foreman remembered the name of carpenter Joseph of village Nazareth in Galilee. Yes, of course, the foreman recalled that his work had been excellent. Unfortunately though, Jesus learned upon arrival, there was one complication. The foreman could not hire Jesus, even for a few months of work. Herod's interest had shifted from the completion of the Jerusalem project to construction of a sumptuous winter capital in tropical Jericho. While there would be no work forthcoming in Jerusalem, there was opportunity at the site of work in Jericho. There would be no problem, for the foreman had connections.

Carpenter Jesus was disappointed. He regarded it compromise enough to subject his skill to the reign of Herod. The one redeeming feature of his initial plan was that Herod or no Herod, it was at the temple of the Most High that he had planned to serve. He would devote his skills to enhancing the temple. What similar satisfaction could he derive from employment at Herod's palace in Jericho? The foreman, pious son of Israel that he was himself, was sympathetic to this reservation, but urged Jesus to relax his principles and make his way toward Jericho.

"When your father first came to work on the temple, he was like you. He was anxious for marriage, with not much experience and with great innocence. He did not recognize the difference between ginkgo and sycamore. He was thorough in all he learned and not only made enough for a dowry, but he also acquired a trade. It can be that way for you.

"Friend, consider the responsibilities to wife and family that you are preparing to undertake. These are hard times for the people. I do not need a Galilean to tell me that Herod is more Roman than Jewish. But what is Israel if not a nation of survivors? Your responsibility to Israel is to raise a family. The Most High looks the other way at the compromises we all make as we wait for the Messiah to appear among us. Go to Jericho. Build walls and ceilings in the capital of Herod; and, as you do, pray the Most High to come to our assistance and make haste to help us."

Jesus was persuaded. Even though there was no work for him in Jerusalem, in another place construction work was moving apace and to there he would travel. There was no grave reason why he should not make the effort to go to a place where he had never been, to carry with him the recommendation from the foreman that would have impressed upon it the seal of the temple. There was no reason why he should not present himself in Jericho at the site of winter headquarters of King Herod. To rich and fertile Jericho, 15 miles to the north and east of Jerusalem, Jesus would travel.

"Give the devil his due," many said of Herod, for the road to Jericho was kept in good repair. It was a steep and winding way that spiraled always downward from the heights of the exalted city of Jerusalem, more than 2,000 feet above sea level, to the lush and spring-nurtured oasis city Jericho, below the water of the earth. A strong and willing beast was needed for a traveler to make the trip, and even then, the going could be expected to be arduous. Jesus would not want his beast to lose footing and perish over the side of the road. Level stretches of earth would need to be found in order to sleep in the afternoon. The road had dangers more perilous than steepness. It was notorious for thievery and assault.

The journey was even slower than had been expected. The winter rains had been heavy and occasionally the road had been washed away. Streams, too, were high and fast. At least there would be no problem with water. Both beast and owner needed to be exceedingly cautious when making a detour over the face of a hill to a place where they could rejoin the road. As Jesus continued the descent, he marveled at the lush vegetation. As beautiful a sight as this, he thought, was not rivaled by anything he had ever seen in beautiful Galilee.

Traveling for a few hours he realized that this day the sun would be a formidable opponent. Only a fool would drive a beast too hard in such heat. Better to proceed slowly and take water and rest sensibly. Both beast and rider would need a well-shaded place to take shelter from the zenith. After sleep and rest, he continued and now his beast covered the distance more quickly. Soon he would be in Jericho.

These were his thoughts when it began, first as sound, then as sight. There was a rustle and then time stopped as the sun seemed to stand still before his eyes for one long moment. After these, events occurred faster than he could record them in his mind.

He had been negotiating a sharp turn in the road when someone jumped from a tree upon him. At first the beast accelerated its speed, but between the steepness of the terrain, the narrow road and the impact of the added weight, it lost balance, and its legs buckled in a panicked response to the crisis. The beast sensed what needed to be done. It deposed both master and brigand without hesitation. Once free of its double burden, it took off at breakneck speed and vanished down the road, leaving carpenter Jesus alone in peril with neither beast nor neighbor. At this time, two others emerged from their concealment in the shrubbery and the onslaught against this unprotected traveler who had been convinced to proceed to Jericho not for Herod but for Israel, began in earnest.

As it occurred, Jesus tried to concentrate on the details. How many were there? At the time he thought there were two, but later he would be certain that there were three. What did they look like? That he could not describe. He did remember that the clubbing and the cruelty were relentless. Against three, defense was useless. When he cried out it was only to have them mock his Galilean accent. Suddenly, he was not a man of Israel, en route to Jericho for employment, hoping to earn silver enough for a dowry bag. Now he was a boy again, far from the protection of mother Miriam and father Joseph. He was alone. Now he was frightened.

As one held him down to the ground, another pressed a knife to his throat and the last of them reached for the sack attached to Jesus' girdle in which coins were carried. Disappointed with their meager recompense for their morning's labor, one of the thieves said, "Enough with this wretched Galilean. He is not worth our while." Having taken all from

Jesus, that is, his dignity, his coins and his beast, the thieves left this bloodied mess for likely death, while they went off to select a site from which they would stage their next ambush. Perhaps the next victim would be prosperous.

As the morning sun continued its ascendancy toward the zenith, victim Jesus lapsed in and out of consciousness. Whenever he did revive, it was only to the awareness of the pool of blood in which he lay. He was bleeding profusely from both head and side. In the sky above, he saw carrion assemble. He prayed: "Most High! May heaven hold them accountable for what they have done to me."

Then coming from the distance, he heard the soft sounds of singing:

> How I love your palace,
>   The Most High Sabaoth!
> How my soul yearns and pines
>   for the Most High's courts!
> My heart and my flesh sing for joy
>   to the living God (Ps 84:1-2).

"What can this be?," Jesus thought. "Yes, it is singing. Someone is passing. It is help that has come."

Yes, though Jesus could not be sure how much time had elapsed, someone was passing. It was a Levite on his way to join in an orchestral ensemble in the temple precincts. As he made his way, the Levite continued the pilgrimage song:

> Happy those who live in your house
>   and can praise you all day long;
> and happy the pilgrims inspired by you
>   with courage to make the Ascents!

> As they go through the Valley of the Weeper,
>   they make it a place of springs.
> They make their way from height to height
>   soon to be seen before God on Zion (Ps 84:4-7).

From the side of his saddle pack hung the six-stringed lyre which the wind made hum. Noticing victim Jesus, the Levite halted his beast. "This man is dead," he thought. That being the case, he judged it better to continue traveling, and, at all costs, not to touch him. His journey was important, for this Levite was scheduled to perform in the temple ensemble during the next few days. To touch the dead would bring impurity upon him and upon his music. For impurity he would be pronounced ineligible for service before the Most High. Thus, with fear that his music might be deemed unacceptable, the Levite continued the trek up to Jerusalem and to the city of the Most High. There his music would be undefiled, and his purity untroubled. Jesus realized that the Levite had decided not to stop. As he drifted into unconsciousness, he heard the Levite continue the hymn to the Most High:

> The Most High Sabaoth, hear my prayer,
> listen, God of Jacob;
> God, our shield, now look on us
> and be kind to your anointed.

> A single day in your courts
>   is worth more than a thousand elsewhere;
> merely to stand on the steps of God's house is
>   better than living with the wicked (Ps 84:8-10).

Some time later a priest happened along. Like the Levite, his destination was also the temple. He was of Aaron's line and it was the week for his section of priesthood to fulfill its turn before the altar of the Most High. He certainly had no time for tending to a roadside casualty. In fact, before he reached Jerusalem, he could expect to see three or four more of these cases. Best to hasten, before he became one. Like the Levite before him, he considered the contamination. After all, this could be the time when the lots fell to him. If he were pure, it would be his privilege now to enter the sanctuary, to take the liturgical silver into his hands and offer the sacrifice of incense to the Most High. For that, surely purity would be essential. With blood in such abundance, ritual defilement would be a certainty. Nothing for this priest of the Most High to do but continue without interruption.

Victim Jesus was showing the signs of shock. Though the sun was at its zenith now and the air was humid and hot, the victim was beginning to shiver. Respiration was both rapid and shallow and his pulse was accelerated and weak. The periods of consciousness, both more brief and less frequent, were marked by nausea.

Carpenter Jesus, losing life now, began to pray again with the passions of a dying soul:

> The Most High, God of revenge,
> God of revenge, appear!
> Rise, judge of the world,
> give the proud their deserts!
>
> How much longer are the wicked to triumph?
> Are these evil men to remain unsilenced,
> boasting and asserting themselves? (Ps 94:1-4).

At about this time a Samaritan merchant, packs filled with ivories destined for a Jerusalem merchant, passed along on his way to the city. Though it was not common for anyone to venture into the outdoors in noonday swelter, this Samaritan reasoned that it would be safest for him to travel at this time. Samaritans were fair game for more than thieves. In fact, many Judean rabbis and a portion of the temple establishment in Jerusalem promoted assault upon Samaritans as a form of patriotism and an act pleasing to the Most High. Both Jerusalem and Galilean Jews hated Samaritan apostasy more than Roman supremacy.

Less than a year before there had been an ugly incident in the temple which elevated the Judean and Samaritan controversy to a boiling point. Escaping notice of temple police, Samaritans had entered the sanctuary of the Most High the day before the feast of Passover and desecrated the holy place by strewing bones and skulls of swine across the floor. The sanctuary was violated and the rites of Passover could not be fulfilled that year. That would not be forgotten.

"Give the devil his due," some sympathizers of Herod remarked upon hearing of the sacrilege. "Throughout 46 years of temple construction, neither one service of worship nor one sacrifice was interrupted. Herod was careful about that. Now these heretics whose purity has been defiled by wanton gentile intermingling, can penetrate our guard and blaspheme what is sacred unto us. And our police, with the salaries they draw from the temple treasury, never, but never, see a thing."

The distance of a year had only served further to embitter Jewish contempt for their neighbors to the north. So, yes, it was wise of this Samaritan to make his way at noon. This Samaritan could travel without risk of running into forces anxious for revenge.

The Samaritan saw the victim languishing in the swelter of the sun's heat. Though chances were that this was a trap, still he slowed his beast, halted and cautiously dismounted. Though he had no training in caring for the injured, he knew that this man was close to death. Something immediate needed to be done to halt the profuse bleeding. He arranged the victim's head on a pillow of leaves. Over the ear, attached to the brim of the victim's turban was a curl of wood that identified him as a carpenter. "I wonder if he is married?" the Samaritan thought.

Having landed only yards away, vultures waited impatiently for some signal that their feast could begin. The Samaritan regarded them, but not for long. Taking a stone, he disrupted their congress. "There will be no meal for you today," he shouted as he threw a rock into their midst. Then, bending over Jesus, fearing, like the previous passersby, that at any moment, he, too, would be ensnared in a trap, he realized that this man could not respond.

Jesus' lips moved though as he stirred into consciousness for a moment. Listening carefully, the Samaritan made out from the slow stream of air coming from him, the words of the psalm by which this victim was preparing for death. Yes, death was close. Taking Jesus' hand, the Samaritan wanted him to know that he was not a bandit returning for another strike, but rather that he was his neighbor in these straits. Putting his mouth to Jesus's ear, he recited the end of the same psalm.

> You never consent to that corrupt tribunal
> that imposes disorder as law,
> that takes the life of the virtuous
> and condemns the innocent to death.
>
> No! The Most High is still my citadel,
> My God is a rock where I take shelter (Ps 94:20-22).

Victim Jesus understood that at last help was at hand. The

65

Samaritan reached into the sack fixed to his girdle and took out the vials which contained wine and oil that he carried for such emergencies. He soaked a piece of cloth in the wine and then washed each of the major cuts across the head and side of the victim with this astringent. Again, showing signs of consciousness, victim Jesus winced at the sting.

Next, the Samaritan hoisted Jesus onto his beast; reversing direction, he returned to Jericho. Ivories for the Jerusalem merchant would be delayed for a day or perhaps more.

In Jericho again, he returned to the inn which he had departed only hours before. He and the innkeeper established Jesus in a room upon a thick bed of straw. The Samaritan went searching for a doctor who could properly clean and bind the wounds. The right arm, too, required attention. There was great swelling and it appeared broken.

Upon his return to the inn with a doctor, the Samaritan observed the distress in the eyes of the proprietor. He assumed what was on his mind. The proprietor lost no time in making his own thought clear. Taking the Samaritan out of the hearing of both Jesus and the doctor, the proprietor, knowing that the Samaritan would have to leave soon and resume his trip, stated that he was unwilling to be burdened with this impoverished case. "His recovery will be long and costly," he complained to the Samaritan.

The Samaritan displayed no patience. "This man has been a victim once this day and you will not make him one again. I have been to your inn many times. I have always paid for what I have received here." Then the Samaritan reached into his sack and surrendered to the proprietor 30 coins, more than enough to care for Jesus for weeks. Then he added, "I will return before this is spent. If more is needed for his care, I pledge my word that you will be repaid."

Finishing his work, the doctor seemed encouraged that he was able to stop the bleeding. Victim Jesus was no longer in danger of death. "I cannot tell about the arm," he said with concern. "It is terribly swollen. Perhaps a bone is broken. If that is true, its color will change and the arm will have to be removed. Too bad. What good is a carpenter with only one arm?" But, even with the most optimistic prognosis, he knew it would take time for recovery.

The Samaritan decided that he could leave in a couple of days. During that time the swelling in the arm began to subside. Apparently, it had only been bruised and not broken. The Samaritan was able to resume his journey confident that there was not much cause for worry. The vultures had been robbed of their lunch. This young man would become well. As he took his leave, he promised, "I will come again."

There was one more matter to which he needed to turn his attention before he left Jericho. The Samaritan went to an acquaintance in the Roman legion's garrison in that city and made arrangements for a detail to be mounted and go to Nazareth to notify the man's family, for, he rightly reasoned, they had a right to know what had occurred and that their son was recovering. "Besides," thought the Samaritan with some mischief, "what is the good of having all these Romans around if you can not bribe one to mount a steed and carry a message across the countryside?"

In this inn during the next few weeks carpenter Jesus felt his strength return and soon he was walking the streets of Jericho. He had much time to consider the kindness of the Samaritan who had risked so much to save his life and invested so much of his own resources upon his recovery.

During the days he explored Jericho, thinking that even though he had traveled extensively throughout Galilee, and even though he had been to Jerusalem for the feasts of the Most High on some occasions, he had never seen the likes of this city before. "Yes," he thought to himself, "though the Most High prefers Zion, surely Herod prefers Jericho, and not without reason." Tropical Jericho, so wonderful a place it was, provided refuge from the raw and wet of Jerusalem winters. Here the winter was an innocent thing that abdicated to early spring.

The inn was grandeur itself. It was a large accommodation whose walls were made of cut sandstone and whose floors were laid with diamond shaped stones. For Jesus, who before had been familiar with only the simplest of homes, the place seemed like a palace. In all it had 36 rooms, each one opened to the courtyard.

A short distance from the inn was the bath which Herod had built. Jesus passed it each day. It too startled his eyes and embarrassed his imagination. The walls around the baths were plastered and painted red, black and gold. Going inside, he saw that its floors were set in mosaic stones. Its warm, spring-fed waters swirled as the conversation of the wealthy and powerful of Jericho swirled, too, in endless circles. Everywhere Jesus turned in Jericho, he met supply and luxury. Even the homes of those in this Roman colony boasted of cellars in which they stored Mediterranean wines as well as boxes for perfumed butters.

Yes, Jericho was a place more developed than he had ever seen. The chief reason for this was reached by following an imposing grand staircase that led to the upper levels of the city and to the complex of government buildings that comprised Herod's winter capital.

After a few weeks Jesus was well enough to begin working on the construction of the palace of Herod. Still, there often the work was halted while all awaited shipments of either paint or sandstone. During those times, Jesus would wander through the streets of Jericho and explore the shoreline of the river.

During his long period of recovery Jesus considered the architecture and wealth of the place and enjoyed its climate. Often he reflected on his narrow escape from death and of the unexpected kindness from the Samaritan to whom he owed life and limb.

Behind Jericho was a stark mountain, on which, legend had it, Satan prowled. In the other distance was the snow-covered Mount Hermon. Upon its peak, snows never melted. Jesus decided that when well enough he would roam the wilds of that mountain and there fast and pray in thanksgiving for his life and salvation from the grave, even if it meant the chance of meeting Satan. No, he did not much believe in rumors. Two weeks later, he set off in the direction of Horeb. There on Horeb he fasted in thanksgiving for his life and for his salvation from the grave.

It was only there, on Horeb itself, that he could under-stand the legends that on that stark mountain Satan roamed freely in search for someone to devour. Yes, there was eeriness and forsakenness that could evoke thoughts not of the Most High but of Satan.

There, far from Jericho's favors, one was vulnerable to temptation. A hungry person, or one who during the day had too much of sun and not enough of water, or one who had drunk sand instead of milk, could see the stones and wish that they be made loaves of bread. Or, looking over ledges upon the panorama might make a poor man greedy for wealth, or a man who had been as deeply shaken as had Jesus, arrogant enough to desire revenge. Yes, from that vantage, one would want all: ownership of the world.

As he crossed the stark mountain, Jesus sought to dismiss these thoughts and considered instead the mercy that had been his because of the compassionate Samaritan. Leaving Horeb and returning to Jericho, Jesus realized that perhaps more than life, perhaps soul as well had been saved by this neighbor. Yes, Jesus was changing.

True to his word, the Samaritan returned after a number of weeks and was heartened to see carpenter Jesus so thoroughly recovered. "Blessed be the Most High," he exclaimed, "for he raises the dead."

During the next days carpenter Jesus tried to persuade the Samaritan to return with him to Galilee where he could meet mother Miriam and father Joseph. This the man would not hear.

"You are young, yet," he said, "and you do not understand. There is not yet enough peace between Judea and Samaria," he said. "Perhaps someday there will be. Then I will visit."

Jesus was impressed by the wisdom of the Samaritan, but, by it Jesus was also disheartened. How foolish seemed the ancient enmity between Judea and Samaria. In farewell to the Samaritan, he said, "Blessed be the Most High, for he is over us all, Judean and Samaritan." And the Samaritan added, "Blessed be the Most High, he makes us neighbors to one another."

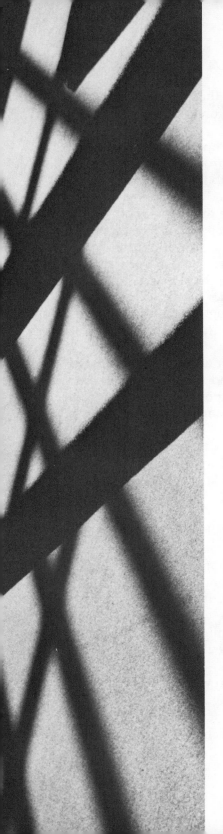

6

Birthday for Herod But Not for John

Herod had John chained up in prison because of Herodias, his brother Philip's wife whom he had married.

(Mark 6:17)

As far as royal houses went, the one of the Herods was not of any ancient duration. Only three times had it provided rulers for Israel. Though it aspired to great sovereignty and service, it was dogged with opposition both from above and below. However true it was that substantial largesse from the imperial treasury of Rome supported this monarchy and hoped at inspiring the people to support it as well, the Caesars of Rome regarded the house of the Herods as agents who were to act in every instance for the best interests of the empire. What Rome hoped for in return for its funding was docility from impoverished Israel and Judea that had neither much of goods or of services to contribute to the prosperity of the empire. In addition, these people had a reputation for being hard to manage, fond of waging war and ambitious for better borders.

In some ways, the largesse was Rome's poor investment, for the people of Israel and Judea regarded these Herods as foreign opportunists insensitive both to their piety and their intense desire for freedom. And all the Roman coins the Herods distributed did little to change this impression. In the opinion of those they ruled, the Herods were a foreign house.

For 60 years one man had served this royal household of the Herods. When he was barely a teen, he had been abandoned on the streets of Jericho. Herod the Great, king of the Jews, was passing through those tropics on a royal progress, and upon noticing him hungry and neglected, included him in his household. It was for acts like this that Herod would praise himself.

As this wraith grew into maturity and now advanced age, his authority within Herod's house had widened with responsibility. King Herod grew to depend upon the man's judgment and loyalty and to yield to his persuasions. He stabilized Herod's rocky reign as well as his rocky personality.

In years past, it was the old man who had dispatched to Rome when they were teens three of King Herod's sons for safekeeping. He convinced a reluctant king of the wisdom of this by explaining that a few years in Rome could only serve the Judean realm.

"They have a measure of your wisdom and cleverness, O king!" he persuaded. "In Rome, they will see great imperial buildings and return home with the grandest of designs for your highness to consider. And their hands will be filled with tribute from ambitious senators and lieutenants. And in the capital of the empire, they will become well known by equals to their rank and station. And surely mighty Caesar himself will develop an interest in them for they are sons of King Herod."

The boys had arrived upon the age when passion goes unrivaled for the attention of the young, so, to them, the old man's approach was somewhat different. It was one that appealed to the anti-Semitic blood which they had inherited two generations ago from their Idumean grandfather, the first of all Herods, the Antipater.

"My young men, my young men," the old man began, "nice people, these sons and daughters of Israel, but surely you are aware of how intolerant they are about matters of the flesh. Remember, you are princes, and in Rome women know that princes are not to be denied all they seek. A few years of this sort of living, far away from the too-easy-to-scandalize eyes and wagging tongues of your father's subjects, will be best for you."

The old man, of course, had reasons of his own, which had little to do with either architecture or promiscuity, reasons that had convinced him of the need for these three to be gone far from father's eye and father's suspicion. King Herod's control was slipping badly. Whenever it did, the drawing of family blood was his solution. In weeks and months of late, there had been fresh blood on the hands of King Herod. He had already killed sons Alexander and Aristobulus, wife Mariamne, brother Joseph, and assorted brothers-in-law. While his original method of preference had been drowning, recently he had turned to poison as the gruesome method.

The old man reasoned that if the dynasty was to continue, that if this house which, for all of King Herod's slaughter, had done much for the prosperity of Israel was to continue, it would be the task of one of these sons. Certainly, it would be crucial then to keep them clear of harm's way, that is, far from the path of their rampaging father. And, no doubt, the knowledge of Latin and of the poets of the Romans would serve them in later years when it came to be their turn to rule.

Now, 60 years since this wraith had been stolen from the streets of Jericho, he was still in the service of the royal house. King Herod had long since died and the land he ruled had been divided among his sons. Herod Antipas was the second Herod whom the old man served.

It was Antipas' judgment that for all his loyalty to Rome, he had never been appropriately recognized. Though he longed to have his father's title, king of the Jews, it had never been conferred on him. On this matter of title, he was becoming more and more frustrated. The old man understood Antipas well enough to know how dangerous this could be. For Antipas' judgment was often wrong.

Antipas had just returned from a diplomatic mission to Mesopotamia on behalf of Tiberius Caesar who sought an alliance between the empire and friendly Artabanes, king of the Medes. The value of alliance with this throne from which long ago great Darius of Persia had reigned was not lost on the Roman emperor. Though an ambassador of Caesar named Vitellius had formally headed this diplomatic mission, Antipas was prominent in the entourage. Tiberius had asked him to spy, a service Antipas often provided, and one which he accomplished skillfully.

With the mission to Artabanes completed and successful, en route to Rome, the caravan passed along the edge of Antipas' domain. At his importuning, the mission stopped at Machaerus, an isolated fortress on the Salt Sea that King Herod had rebuilt. The prince had promised them a feast there to celebrate the new alliance between Rome and Persia, an alliance which Vitellius had forged, but one which Antipas, to accommodate his own interest in flattering Caesar, had already compromised with Artabanes through bribes and flattery. And it was the preparations for this banquet which now wholly occupied Antipas.

Here was his plan. There at the banquet he would proclaim himself king of the Jews. Though it would be a bold move to make, Antipas was confident that in Rome Tiberius would be so pleased with the successful mission to Artabanes that he would excuse it. "This Caesar likes courage and awards confidence," Antipas thought. With the unfolding of such a delicate event on his mind, naturally, the prince did not want to be reminded when the old man came and offered counsel about a religious prisoner, one who, by coincidence, was incarcerated there at Machaerus, in a cistern dungeon.

His name was John and he was of the priest tribe. Years of prayer and fasting in the desert at the monastery of the Essenes had made of John a stark figure. But something impelled him to leave the desert and return among the people. He preached to them the fire and judgment that had been shown to him in the wilderness and of which he claimed that now the time was near. He had been preaching at Bethany at the shallow ford of the Jordan and had received a great response from the people who were always anxious to give a new prophet a hearing.

It was not only excitement about the apocalypse that John had created, he had also created mischief. He was sly enough to rekindle a cause of popular resentment, the controversial topic of Antipas' divorce and adulterous marriage to Herodias, his brother Philip's wife. His wife had only contempt for this accuser. To please her, Antipas had John imprisoned, but intended to free him after a suitable period of time during which he hoped his wife's anger might subside and during which the people's fancy might be captured by the next prophet to appear at the river.

In both matters, Antipas had misjudged both the depth of his wife's anger and the people's respect for John. Now it was a year later and John's continued confinement neither satisfied Herodias nor wearied the loyalty of the Jews. Herodias remembered. Keeping her acute bitterness for his accusations against her, she yelled to her husband to exact revenge. And the people remembered. In their high regard for this prophet of righteousness, they yelled for his freedom. Since the situation never improved, John's imprisonment continued as a stalemate which tangled together the Jewish people, their would-be king and his illicit wife in a hopeless knot.

While Antipas was on his diplomatic mission of espionage and intrigue, the old man was dutifully at home, keeping watchful eye on all developments. Upon the return of the prince the old man urged him to decide on the matter of John. The years had taken from the old man his persuasive and diplomatic manner. No longer was he the soothing and unctuous counsellor who could persuade the king. Now he was more like an old dog. He said, "The title a faraway Caesar sets on your head will mean nothing. Satisfy your people now with the release of the one they call the Baptist. All regard him as a prophet, and for some he is the Messiah. Order your wife's submission to a husband's and a prince's authority."

Having heard the old man speak about affairs of the realm before with similar conviction, Antipas thought too much was being made of this matter. Yet he faulted himself for having let the situation continue unaddressed for as long as it had. Best to handle it now, and end it swiftly.

"Even a prophet has a price," he said to the old man. "You are to go to John. Have him carried by mule from the dungeon in which he has been confined. A year of stench and darkness should have weakened his resistance to my adultery. Have him taken to the hot springs nearby where Great Herod my father died. Then bring in a Bedouin maid to anoint his skin with oil. Make her perfume his entire body and comb his hair and beard. She will know what next to do. Prophets not only have voice, old man, prophets have flesh, as well. Then, when she has satisfied him and he is sweetly smelling and anointed, you go and see him.

"He came from the desert, they say. Tell John that Antipas has ruled that he is to return to the desert. Inform John that Antipas will raise a monastery in the wilderness to rival that place for piety in which he lived. In the monastery of Antipas, the devout will be able to pursue the reign of the Most High without either distraction or discomfort. Tell John that he will be appointed father of this monastery for a term of office not to expire before his death. Tell John that he and his monks will never be in need for either food or oil, for either scrolls or linen, for as long as a Herod reigns from the exalted throne of my grandfather. If it is zealous for the Most High that this prophet wants to be, let him be zealous for the Most High in the desert."

"Antipas, I regret I sent you off to Rome," the old man answered. "Though you know Virgil, you do not know the dreams of Daniel. John is a man who has received the Spirit of the Most High and he will not be bought, not by a Bedouin whore, a desert monastery, not by all the silver coins which you have struck and on which you have embossed your own name and, mercy on me, Antipas, for what I say, your own countenance.

"John is a prophet without a price," the old man continued. "He is well-considered by the people. While your horses carry you on royal progresses to where your spying and intrigue will ingratiate you with Caesar, this nation seethes with anger against your house. Your grandfather was a foreigner, and, in the minds of the people, he was no Jew at all. This people knows you well. They know your Latin poets and your Roman dress. They know your diet that disregards the prescriptions of the law, your fornication with the daughters of Israel, and mercy again on me, Antipas, for what I say, the bed to which you have taken your own brother's wife."

Antipas would ignore him. "Unlike other rulers, why cannot I have servants who speak respectfully to their prince?" said Antipas as he dismissed the old man from his chamber. Yes, Antipas permitted the old man to speak in a fashion in which no other living person could. Again, he was certain, all this concern was excessive. This day Antipas could only be concerned about tomorrow's feast and the proclamation for which he hoped.

Now he went to supervise those preparing the banquet. This matter of the Baptist was nothing, he assured himself. As in all things, nothing hasty could be done. He had presented the obvious solution to the old man and to his point of view the old man would arrive as he usually did. The establishment of a monastery in the desert was a small price if it meant returning a prophet who had strayed from his proper environment back to the wilderness where he belonged, and, at the same time, if it calmed an oversensitive wife's pride.

With the matter of John decided upon, he considered the announcement that would make him king. He had planned it carefully in his mind. His wife's daughter, Salome, would lead a troupe of dancers and delight the visitors from Rome. He would make the arrangements with her. At the end of her dance, it would occur.

The dance would do it all. First, the music would have a plaintive and haunting quality, marked by the evocative sounds by which wind instruments speak. So delicate, so innocent and so subtle would she be at first that listeners would hardly notice that the tempo had become enlivened as string instruments began to dominate. But by the time that this occurred, it would be too late. To the higher music of the strings the girl would present herself, all hands and palms, all neck and back, extending her body in every direction.

77

As the music heightened, who would notice the competition between flames from the lanterns and the flames from their own passion? Though they would rise from their couches and stand higher than the flames, the dancing stepdaughter would remain the dominant flame. In one final crescendo of display, the music and the dance would end abruptly and she would fall to the earth exhausted, completing the ruin by lust of those who had watched it all. Then her face would be raised and she would summon from somewhere within a look that confessed, slyly, that she was seeking now from them forgiveness for what she had so deliberately set out to accomplish.

Antipas, too, would appear to be overwhelmed by this. His own body would shiver. But this would be in careful check and he would not allow his passion to change his plan. Oh no, nothing would change this plan, this great plan for him to be declared king. If anything, it would serve it. In Antipas, ambition was stronger than passion.

Yes, Antipas thought, this would do just fine. This would be the plan. When his stepdaughter had finished, he would demand the attention of the entire house of guests and then to her say, "Daughter of Herodias, to you I will give anything you ask, even to half my kingdom."

And she would say, "O husband of my mother! I ask only one favor. I ask that you declare yourself 'king of the Jews.' "

To serve this request, would not Antipas be obliged? Would there be a choice? After the oath to which he had sworn — remember it was to half the realm — he would have to be obliged. The declaration would be made as the stepdaughter and dancer of the night — all carnal will that she was — had wished.

Antipas would declare himself king of the Jews and at this the guests would applaud. Caesar in Rome, when he would hear of it, he too would applaud. Remember, this Caesar liked courage and rewarded confidence. Yes, Antipas was satisfied as he considered the plan. Tomorrow, he would be king of the Jews.

But as Antipas was anticipating the dance of his stepdaughter, the conversation he had with the old man was being reported to wife Herodias by the slave who spied for her. Now

Herodias swiftly considered plans other than her husband's and set off immediately in the direction of her daughter.

In a hidden scabbard Herodias had kept a silver knife that her father-in-law, Great Herod, had given her on the occasion of her marriage to her first husband, Herod Philip. Now it was her mind's turn to compose the scene of the dance. Yes, she too developed her plan and after the Baptist's head was on a platter, she would spear his slanderous tongue with its silver blade. And that would be one prophet's tongue that would never flap again in judgment against her bed.

And, O yes! she smiled as a final thought entered her mind. She would have him buried in a field in hated Samaria.

7

At Cana a Wedding Feast Is Saved

People generally serve the best wine first, and keep the cheaper sort till the guests have had plenty to drink; but you have kept the best wine till now.

(John 2:10)

He would travel to Cana and attend the wedding feast. He would travel to Cana because his mother had asked him to be present. Father Joseph had died during Passover. Upon a father's death, what in Israel could rank as more important than obedience to one's mother?

Ill all year, father Joseph had been unable to travel that spring with son or wife to Jerusalem for the feast. That had concerned this man who in his own way during his life had practiced obedience to the Most High.

"Every faithful son of Israel is to keep Passover in Jerusalem," father Joseph admonished himself before the son. "May the Most High have mercy on my absence."

But to this, son Jesus had a swift

answer. "My father, rabbis teach that during the feast the boundaries of Jerusalem are expanded so the homes of the sick and the caves of lepers are included, no matter how far from the city they might be. My father, our teachers have pronounced upon it: you, too, worship in Jerusalem this year."

Father Joseph, moved by this wisdom, placed his hands upon the son's head in blessing. "Next year in Jerusalem, my Jesus," he whispered, and kissed the son softly on the head.

This was the final blessing and the last kiss Jesus would receive from father Joseph. This man, who was not old, died that year during the days of the feast in Jerusalem. Shortly after this, Jesus had realized it was time for him to leave his home. His mother had understanding enough to respect his intention, even if she was not adept in explaining to friends and relations the abrupt departure of an unmarried son from the side of a widowed mother. Advice from them all was forthcoming: "You are a widow and by the law can demand your son's obedience, yet you allow him to leave you unprovided for?"

It had been nearly a year since the father had died and another Passover was at hand. Before the annual trek to Jerusalem, first there would be a visit to Cana, nine miles distant from Nazareth, for a wedding feast.

Much had been done to ready Cana for these observances, for in all ways this union was to be as the law provided. Father Moses had prescribed that the groom be at least 13 years and one day in age, and the woman, 12 and one-half years. So it was. Moses had provided that before marriage, a betrothal would first be arranged according to precept and tradition. So it was. Earlier in the year, a contract between the fathers had been notarized. Then the bride price, consisting of a bag of silver shekels, a handsome parcel of land and a fine gold ring, had been given to the father of the bride.

Again, as required before a wedding, bride and groom were to abstain from food. For at times of importance both father David and father Moses had fasted and prophet Daniel, too, had given this example. The Pharisees, who vigorously recommended this devotion, said that fasting was good for both soul and heart, not to mention belly. As it was required, for nine days prior to the wedding, bride and groom would not from sunrise to sunset partake of either food or beverage. Now nine days had elapsed and the days of fasting had come to term. The wedding drew near.

As was the custom for most weddings, it would take an entire week for the people of this town to fulfill the specifications of father Moses and their own requirements for joy. Throughout the preparations, a careful and fastidious governor of the feast had been at work. No one could accuse him of not knowing how the system worked. For example, the commanding centurion of the Roman cohort assigned to keep Cana obedient was an officer easily corrupted by a bag of silver or by a rich meal. Weeks before, the bribe had been presented to him by the governor. Yes, troops would be kept clear of this wedding crowd.

"There will be no trouble here and no talk of rebellion. For sons and daughters of Israel, a wedding is like the sabbath," the governor, somewhat overdoing himself, explained convincingly to this gentile. "During it, Israel forgets all else because it considers itself as having passed, if even briefly, into eternity." Even if the centurion did not fully accept the story, he accepted the bribe.

Next the governor turned attention to the groom's house. There he presided in demanding fashion over preparation of foods and construction of the outdoor booths that would shelter the guests in case of bad weather. "May the Most High show forth his power over this Cana sky," he said each time he thought of the rapid formation of a storm coming to them from the lake.

First, his workers would transform the groom's home into a synagogue. Benches would be arranged in the center of its inner court. These were the places for the men. Around the edge the women and children would stand. Yes, he thought, everyone would fit. If needed, neighboring rooftops would serve as a gallery. It might be as crowded as the temple during the holy days, but everyone would be accommodated. And delight of delights, in front of the benches was the great booth of marriage, the *huppah*. The booth was the shelter under which the couple and the rabbi stood during the ceremony.

For the preparation of the *huppah*, ass-drawn carts carrying flowers gathered from the fields and gardens of Cana arrived at the groom's house. Their colorful burden included saffron croci, many kinds of narcissus, red anemone and lavender mimosa blossoms, and the long-lived yellow and pink flowers of laurel. It was the task of Cana girls and boys to adorn the *huppah* with flowers. The poorest could only afford a canopy of flowers and during the wedding it was supported by the four poles which unmarried men held. In this village, the *huppah* would be a booth with three walls and a roof. The governor directed the excited children to obey him and perform their task in a most responsible fashion: "Little matter how symbolic this flowered shelter is," he instructed, "it will be, according to Moses and the traditions of Israel, the first home of a husband and wife of Israel; and, as such, it stands as chosen before the Most High."

All seemed to be in readiness. Everything, including six large stone jars stood ready for the water that would purify the knives and kettles, or any person who, by misfortune, might have brushed against either a gentile or a woman who was in her period. Nothing had been left to chance, nothing, that is, except the supply of wine. Nor had that important feature been neglected. It would be more accurate to explain that this was left to the kindness of the guests, for custom dictated that wine for the feast be provided by the invited. As the days of the feast were about to begin, work in the fields was halted, the hum of spinning wheels was silenced, and the heavy fumes from the tanning tubs departed from the air.

Cana was ready for celebration. Even donkeys and asses had been decorated with small bells, crimson ribbon and shells. Invited guests and family from other places, too, had begun to assemble. On the streets were heard the joyful sounds that are made when, after a long time, brother and brother, and sister and sister meet and note how parents have aged, how the young have matured and how more enfeebled aunts or uncles have become. Of course, mother Miriam and Jesus would be received with many condolences. "Yes, it was last year during Passover. May the Most High be merciful," mother and son would say in acknowledgment over and again to the offering of the sympathies of friends and relations.

"Blessed be the Most High," friends and relations would answer. "He calls all to judgment."

Jesus had arrived in Cana on Wednesday with the men and women who had begun to travel in his company. The day of their arrival the observances began as the men gathered in the home of the groom for rejoicing with him. Then, after darkness fell and the groom was dressed, all formed the procession that would carry the groom from his home to that of the bride. It was the business of men alone to provide an escort for the groom.

Thus amid much rejoicing they carried the groom who was dressed in the gorgeous white shawl with blue tassels that was customary attire for this first night of the wedding feast. Upon his head he wore a crown that the men of his family had worn at their weddings throughout the generations of Israel. They carried him on a litter through the streets to the acclaim of the people. Young cousins carried tall sticks with torches at the top. The groom distributed small pieces of sweetmeats to the children as he went. Light was all important at a wedding.

"This day," someone shouted from a rooftop to him as he passed, "you are king of Israel."

And en route the escort sang the ancient song of the people:

> What is this coming up from the desert
> like a column of smoke,
> breathing of myrrh and frankincense
> and every perfume the merchant knows?
>
> See, it is the litter of Solomon.
> Around it are sixty champions,
> the flower of the warriors of Israel;
> all of them skilled swordsmen,
> veterans of battle (Sg 3:6-7).

Once arrived, the 20 bridesmaids who had waited for a long time, now forgot their ordeal of patience and met the 60 champions and their groom at the door with their torches burning. The groomsmen greeted the maids.

> Daughters of Zion
> come and see King Solomon,
> wearing the diadem
> with which his mother crowned him
> on his wedding day,
> on the day of his heart's joy (Sg 3:11).

They presented the groom to the father of the bride who looked pleased. First he welcomed him and then escorted him into the home where his daughter waited. The bride was dressed in blue. Golden rounds adorned her forehead. Her mother and her sisters attended her. Her mother wore pink. Then the bride, too, was enthroned on a litter. Bride and groom were carried through the streets back to the groom's home.

Now it was the maids' turn for acclaim. "This day," they cried to her, "you are queen of Israel." An old woman said, "Blessed be the Most High, he renews Israel with marriage."

The groom sang to his bride.

> How beautiful you are, my love,
> Your eyes, behind your veil, are doves;
> your hair is like a flock of goats
> frisking down the slopes of Gilead.
> Your lips are scarlet thread
> and your words enchanting.
> Your cheeks, behind your veil,
> are halves of pomegranate.
> Your neck is the tower of David
> built as a fortress
> hung round with a thousand bucklers,
> and each the shield of a hero.
> You are wholly beautiful, my love (Sg 4:1,3-4,7).

By this time, in the groom's home, the assembly of Israel had gathered. The rabbi began the ritual of marriage by reciting the benediction from the Torah: "Blessed are you, O Lord our God! the Most High, for you have created joy and gladness, bride and bridegroom, mirth and exaltation, pleasure and delight, love, brotherhood, peace and fellowship. Soon, O

Lord God! may there be heard in the cities of Judah, and in the streets of Jerusalem, the voice of joy and gladness, the voice of the bridegroom and the voice of the bride, the jubilant voice of bridegrooms from canopies, and of youths from their feasts of song. Blessed are you, O Lord God! the Most High, who makes this bridegroom to rejoice with the bride."

Next, from a scroll there was a reading about Noah and the flood. When the reader had finished the task, all stood to hear the teaching. Seating himself, the rabbi assumed the posture of teacher in Israel. He taught thus on the meaning of marriage:

"Little children," he said, "we have heard of our father Noah and the ark of rescue. The Most High chose the humble marriages of Noah and his children to be the beginning of the new kingdom that receives the blessedness intended for all from the beginning.

"The great promise of the marriage of Noah and his wife enlightens us to know the meaning of marriage between faithful sons and daughters in Israel. For, two by two, boarding the ark of marriage, bride and groom inaugurate that kingdom which the Most High desires, the new creation restored to all blessedness and to every peace."

Then the rabbi explained that marriage was exaltation and election and that it was the renewal of earth and heaven itself. He said that the Most High crowns marriage in Israel by the upbringing of children who fear the Most High and uphold the law.

"Your children," he said, "will be your greatest achievement. To your children you will entrust your good land and your good name and through them the story of Israel will be told unto the generations."

Then the rabbi led the bride seven times around the groom. As the groom placed the wedding ring on the bride's finger, he repeated, as the rabbi directed, ancient words: "Behold you are consecrated to me by this ring according to the law of Moses and of Israel."

All retired to the banquet area while family and guests began a full and lavish meal. The bride and groom withdrew, going for the first time as husband and wife to their house. In their absence the celebration continued undiminished. Remember how even the beasts bedecked in bells contributed to the gladness. Remember, too, the extravagance of light, for there were lamps everywhere. Wholly beautiful it all was, indeed.

In the morning, bride and groom emerged from their house. The children of Cana faced each other in two long columns of joy as the couple walked through their midst toward the place where festivities had already resumed. As custom required, their path was strewn with seeds and crushed pomegranate. Yes, the children were already wishing them fertility. A day of food and dance, laughter, the proposing of riddles and games began. The young women gathered in the vineyards and the men round-danced with one another. What match would be made for next spring's marriage?

Having demanded everyone's attention, the groom's brother called for a toast and cups were raised. First to the bride, "May you love your husband as you do your own life." Then, to the groom, "May you honor your wife more than you honor your own self." Even the gentile officers of Caesar watched the feast with pleasure, not to mention how they enjoyed the portion of food and drink that the governor provided for them. Yes, well spent was the silver for the bribe. Such joy that day in little Cana!

Who did not agree when an uncle, who had not waited for the toast to partake of the vintage, stood and quoted the proverb with a voice that all Galilee could enjoy: "A wifeless man is a deficient man"?

The meal was splendid. A local herder had sold the parents spring lamb at a price generous to them. Vegetables were in abundance, too, this time of year. Then there were the fruits. There were plums for tartness and figs for sweetness.

Jesus watched mother Miriam move graciously about the crowd, greeting friends and kin. After some time she returned to her son and took him aside, out of the hearing of others.

"They have no wine," she said.

That was the simple way she reported it. She never said more than was needed. In response, he only looked at her and stayed silent. With mother Miriam silence never had effect. So again, she pressed this news on him. "They have no wine." It would be embarrassment for guests and hosts alike. For it meant that many had neglected basic courtesy.

Now he answered. "Woman," he said, "is this a riddle you propose for me to answer?" Then, seeing the seriousness in her eyes, he said, "What can you require of me? I came here because you required my attendance, and, as a widow of Israel, you claim my obedience. In this, what can you demand? Am I Moses that I can strike rock and slake the thirst of the people? My hour has not yet come."

Mother Miriam who did not prefer the indirect discourse of marriage riddles, said directly, "Your hour has come." Having said all she needed, she walked back into the crowd.

Waiters stood nearby. The young of Cana, they, too, were barely 13 and did not know what Miriam knew, that is, they did not know his hour had come.

Jesus came to their circle. "Who among you can recite the riddle our father Samson proposed at his wedding?"

One of them had learned the scriptures better than the rest and answered his question, "The riddle was,

Out of the eater came what is eaten,
and out of the strong came what is sweet" (Jg 14:14).

Jesus approved of the answer and said, "Now I propose a riddle: The jar even though filled was empty."

Even the clever one had no answer for this. Then, as they delighted in the mystery of this riddle, Jesus pointed to the jars standing near to them, jars for purification. "As you think," he directed, "fill these to the top with water, for the rites of purification are now to commence. It is time already to wash away any guilt or uncleanness that there might be here before our father Moses."

The waiters obeyed his order, but were confused. Was it for a guest to call an end to the feast? In fact, the celebration offered no sign of diminishment — remember the uncle who had not waited for the toast to partake in the vintage. Nonetheless, they carried bucket after bucket of water from the well and filled the stone jars. When the last of the six had been filled, Jesus told the youngest of the waiters to draw off a measure and bring it to the governor of the feast and say that this was wine friends and relations from Nazareth had provided.

The governor had been aware of the gravity of the situation. As he observed the amount of wine continue to diminish, he became anxious. When the waiter offered him the measure of clear liquid and urged him to taste, he thought that he was being offered water and became impatient with the interruption. The waiter persisted. When the governor tasted the liquid, he rejoiced. He searched out the groom and asked him to taste the wine.

"Such fine vintage from Nazareth, and so clear?" said the groom, not understanding.

The rejoicing at this wedding would continue undiminished and undepleted. The crisis had passed without one word of it becoming widely known.

The young waiters did not know. Even the one among them who was clever would always remember this as the wedding feast where a riddle was proposed but not solved.

Those who had begun to travel in the company of Jesus knew and left the feast enlightened. The governor, pleased that this crisis had ended, had no intention of discussing it further.

Finally, the widowed mother of Jesus was pleased for the jars of Moses were filled with cold, pure and clear wine of a new kingdom, the kingdom Noah had once served, a kingdom to whose glory these newly married had been elected. All she would do was brush against her son later in the day and exclaim, almost mischievously, "My son, done with such discretion. Father Joseph would have rejoiced."

Yes, on that day, Jesus, with due discretion, did all that was required as a son of Israel and a son of the Most High. That day mother Miriam had been right. For his hour had come.

8

The Woman Who Was a Sinner

She waited behind him at his feet, weeping, and her tears fell on his feet, and she wiped them away with her hair; then she covered his feet with kisses and anointed them with the ointment.

Luke 7:38

It was to be a dinner party and an elegant affair. The list of invited guests was carefully composed to include high echelons of imperial and Judean society. Many officials of Pontius Pilate's administration, on orders from the procurator to improve relations with the Judean establishment, had gladly welcomed this invitation. Late that afternoon, as the hour for the supper approached, messengers went forth in every direction to escort the guests to the place. Once arrived, the assembly of guests was as diverse as it was impressive.

A general of Tiberius' army, having stopped at this imperial outpost, had accepted the invitation. Wearing military dining dress of polished brass and leather, he told long tales of war and victory done for Caesar's sake

in faraway lands and in cities with distance sounding in
their names. In attendance, too, were visiting senators from
Rome. They had traveled to Jerusalem to spy on Herod and to
promise, falsely, aid. They covered their intentions with flattery. Dressed in wool and purple, they spoke in lengthy,
weighty Latin sentences and lamented the costly shopping
their wives had done in every port in which their ships had
docked en route.

Leading priests of the temple, most of whom ranked as
Sadducees, as well as the leadership of the predominately lay
party of Pharisees, had been invited. Though these two did
not usually agree, they had been instructed to set differences
aside and appear united on this night. Merchants, too, had
come with fists bulging with Roman coins, and waiting for an
opportunity to bribe one of Pilate's crowd to look the other way
at one of their schemes or injustices.

The host himself was an important Pharisee named Simon.
Of all the factions that comprised Judean Judaism, the Pharisees boasted to be the most politically astute. As a leader,
Simon spoke for large Pharisee sympathy for Rome. Elo-
quently described was the contempt, expressed by Simon, of
the Judean establishment for fanatic nationalists who promoted
rebellion. Even as the banquet was beginning, his voice of
reason was heard above the din: "We can live with Tiberius,"
he declaimed. "The nation prospers. Herod's temple is more
glorious than was Solomon's, and our synagogues are both
united in their observances and excellent in industry, learnedness and hospitality. We are the envy of gentiles and of the
prophets."

Then to the war hero, Simon said, "Such learnedness
among us, my general, and such advancement. We owe it all
to Rome's beneficence. Inform mighty Tiberius that our nation
is loyal to his reign and appreciative of his many kindnesses."

Simon had hoped for this opportunity, because there was
advantage for him. He hoped that he would be rewarded by
Rome with a title for his praise of the empire. The title he
desired was the one that Pilate himself had received a few
years before. Yes, to be, as Pilate was, a "Friend of Caesar"
was Simon's great ambition.

Poor Simon, there was no telling how this would be reported to Tiberius, for his Latin was coarse and not easily understood. Unfortunately, increased volume did not compensate for the faulty endings which blemished the nouns and verbs that fell from his mouth into the crowd.

But that night the food and wine enjoyed fluency in several languages, for they were as elegant and as fine as the company. Slaves, prisoners of Roman wars, had prepared exotic dishes from their own cities. There too was spread the finest veal that could be purchased from temple butchers. It was served around pistachios which had been roasted. There was citrus and melon, coarse and bitter greens, all of which had been prepared to perfection. There was fenugreek, bells kidney, dormice, and minced nightingale rolled, ah!, in marinated leaves. The fat tails of rams were served. These had been rams whose tails had been so fat that it was required that they be equipped with carriages to support their rear. Of course, there were the fresh sycamore figs which were appreciated for their contribution, sweetness and texture.

However, the most interesting guest was still to arrive. All looked forward to the attendance of Jerusalem's current sensation: carpenter Jesus from Nazareth in Galilee. Though only a craftsman from a poor lake town in the north, he had made quite the stir; first, throughout the fishing villages near his home, Magdala, Capernaum, Cana and Bethseda; and now, on the much more difficult to impress streets of Jerusalem and upon the esplanades of the temple.

These guests knew little of the political or religious message of this Jesus. In fact, some criticized him as being indecisive. Was he zealot or patriot? Some thought he was a prophet. They were undecided how to appraise him. "Yes," one insisted, "he pays tax." "No," another remembered, "he calls Herod a fox." There was general agreement that the goals of his campaign were poorly defined.

However difficult to classify politics, the guests were uniformly impressed by the reports of his magic. What a coup of Simon to have convinced this Jesus to be in attendance. No doubt about it, this Simon was crafty and perhaps a place in Rome might be found for him. All the guests looked forward to seeing Jesus at close range and perhaps persuading him to perform.

The messenger who had gone to escort Jesus returned at last. Jesus arrived with his troop of retainers. Criticizing this motley crowd one said, "It is written, 'You judge a man by the company he keeps.' " Even the Romans there could discern the coarse and guttural accent of these Galileans. Waves of talk and ambition rose and fell again as the wine was poured and guests returned to their conversations and their schemes. Hosted by Simon, Jesus was introduced to the guests.

Many whispered among themselves that they were unsure as to what to think of him. This Jesus seemed difficult and reluctant and certainly not the firebrand of his reputation. Some thought that they had known his type before. He stood there judging and testing the waters, but not committing himself. Still, maintained others, he seemed self-possessed enough. Though the Greek he spoke to slaves and senators was flawless, he would not converse in Latin. One of the senators urged him to do so. Unlike the Pharisees who saw no problem in using the tongue of Judean oppressors, Jesus did. Apparently, he did not hope to be named a "Friend of Caesar." He spoke only Aramaic and Greek that night. With the introductions finished, he was able to leave his host and recline at table and eat. In this he did not disappoint them, for it was said that he loved a good meal.

As was common in homes such as Simon's, a curtain separated the courtyard from the street. Along that wall there was disruption. Apparently someone uninvited had passed through the curtain and was making a way into the banquet.

Commotion, Jesus thought. Perhaps a member of the Zealot party has come to heckle these emperor-minded Pharisees. Almost as soon as this thought had formed, Jesus dismissed it and lowered his eyes. For he realized that, more likely, this was a mother who had arrived to beg bread for a hungry child.

An uninvited woman had arrived. She was there to beg, all right, but for neither bread nor liberty. It was for Jesus that she had come, and from him seeking nothing short of the mercy of God.

Jesus looked at her. She did not wear the customary veil to shroud the features of a woman's face. Hers was a face caked with antimony vermillion rouge that made it red and hot. Her eyebrows were black and her lashes were midnight blue. Her palms, too, had been rendered the product of cosmetics, having been prepared with a henna dye that made them all reddish-yellow. She was making her way toward him.

Spotting him at a table through the crowd, she was determined to push her way; and, before any could prevent her, his palms which had only human color, were raised in a gesture of protection. "Let her alone," he said. Those who had earlier doubted his substance now saw the firebrand.

She fell before him and reached for his feet. Tears fell freely now. Weeping profusely, the woman reverenced his feet over and over with kisses, and wet them with tears. Her hair, antioch-red and plaited like a hive above her head was released. It fell all the distance to her waist. Turning her head at a right angle, she used her hair to wipe away the wetness upon his feet. Then the kissing was resumed. The dust on his feet and the tears from her eyes made salty mud, but for her it was rather like a child's first recognition of sweetness. First pouring, then spilling, costly nard from an alabaster cannister, she anointed. Soon the boldness of her action and the scent of nard overwhelmed room and guests, slaves and cuisine.

Though uninvited, this woman was not unknown. For a long time she had been the manager of her own fame and was better known there than any invited guest. In fact, she was known only too well by some. As righteous as Pharisees and Sadducees were in the light of day, when evening shadows fell, they stole themselves to her house where they waited in the courtyard beyond her door, dressed not in their phylacteries and shawls, but merely wrapped in towels as they waited for her services. There at her place, too, Pharisees and Sadducees set their differences aside. In this fashion had Simon, ambitious though he was for the title "Friend of Caesar," first been designated a friend of hers. Now this Jerusalem whore had come to Simon's house and ruined a dinner, upon the success of which so many national and personal hopes had rested. "Such boldness!" cried Pharisee Simon, all outrage and umbrage, as he moved to push her away from Jesus.

Then, accusing Jesus, he made this demand. "Surely you know what this woman is. Explain how you would let her touch you. And all you pretend to be! Think of the scandal. Tell us, Jesus, are you not aware? Or, tell us, Jesus, are you a friend of hers?"

Then he turned to the guests and, with shock that was the product of no small affectation, said, "My friends! Behold, the upright rabbi is a friend of hers!"

"So what else is new," said one who was not surprised to see the human condition revealed.

No, Jesus had not been her friend; not, that is, in the same way in which Simon and the rest had been. Jesus understood the woman. He realized that she had come to the city orphaned and alone at age 12, at the age when girls her age were receiving a dowry and preparing for marriage. In city alleys she had been raped and beaten. Once she had longed to be the mother of sons of Israel. She had six children, but could not identify one father. And each child she had to give away. That had been the hardest thing, to have given all her children away.

"Simon!" Jesus answered. "I will tell you why her hands reach out to me; but, first, answer this question. If you owed me a hundred coins and I owed you a thousand, and we both canceled the debt, who should be more grateful?"

"You should," Simon answered, "for you had been forgiven a greater debt."

"So it is with her, Simon. What great love in her heart. It is the love rich enough for tears. This daughter of the Most High knows the extent to which she has been forgiven. Be sobered, Simon, by what has been made of her. She is a friend of the Most High our Father. That is why she touches me."

Speaking to the woman, he said, "Your tears have instructed us. Sinners love greatly, as you do, because they have been forgiven much. Therein is the essence of the kingdom." Then the woman left.

The gathering of the highest echelons of imperial and Judean society continued, augmented now by the highest echelons of the kingdom.

9

Woman at the Well of Jacob

He had to cross Samaria. On the way he came to the Samaritan town called Sychar, near the land that Jacob gave to his son Joseph. Joseph's well is there and Jesus, tired by the journey, sat straight down by the well.

(John 4:3-5)

Carrying water was woman's work. It was for a woman to be fitted like an ox with a yoke from which clay jars would hang. It was for a woman to spend her life with calloused neck and stooped spine. This Jesus understood well enough, for to his father's worktable husbands had led their women, much like they had led their beasts, for yokes to be custom-made for their shoulders. Then, too, there had been his mother's routine each morning and afternoon. During dry season she would walk the distance to the village well and return home with water enough for vegetables and laundry and for bathing and drinking. She carried water because walls

97

needed to be washed and hair needed to be combed. She carried enough so that the basil and black cumin that sunned itself on the rooftop would have a drink. She carried water because her husband's feet needed to be washed — and, yes, that was woman's work as well.

At the well she met other women and contributed to the conversation about their men and about their tired bones. On Friday, of course, the burden was twice. Enough water had to be carried on Friday for sabbath, the day on which even woman's work halted.

In the spring this was easier and a more joyful task. For a time during early spring there was not need to go to the well. New rain rushed down mountainsides and coursed through village streams that the men had widened to save the precious thing. The women gathered at the streams and caught the water as it raced along. Long ago their men had built stone steps, fine and great steps indeed, steps deep and stern enough to be recommended even by a Baptist. Upon them women descended into the racing waters to fulfill their responsibilities. Compared to flat cistern water, this was living water. Cold and sweet, it seemed almost lighter for the neck. Collecting this water was a simple thing and your cup ran over.

En route from Judea to Galilee, Jesus told his circle of disciples that they would make the journey through Samaria. To do this, they were wholly reluctant. Jews and Samaritans opposed one another, and, on one occasion not long before this, while passing through Samaria they had been greeted with cruelty because it was known that their destination was Jerusalem. Bitter animosities between the two seemed forever in place. Still, Jesus insisted. They had to pass through Samaria.

"Surely, Rabbi," Simon objected, "though their roads are fine, there are other routes as well. Let us make the journey on the footpaths along the valley Jordan."

No, they would not. They had seen him determined like this before. It was to be through Samaria. Only one of them understood. It was Andrew who said, "Brothers, he has to pass this way."

Usually Jesus did not prefer to travel the roads through the place. The roadways of Samaria led to the sea and exposed its people to Hellenistic ways that were foreign to the ways of the Most High. Wealth had gorged the bazaars of Samaria with goods, notably ivories and other crowns and brooches purchased at Phoenician ports. Had not even Amos condemned these people as having no interest in the progress of the soul?

> Woe to those who feel so safe
> on the mountains of Samaria.
> Lying on ivory beds
> and sprawling on their divans,
> they dine on lambs from the flock,
> and stall-fattened veal;
> they drink wine by the bowlful,
> and use the finest oil for anointing
> themselves,
> but about the ruin of Joseph
> they do not care at all (Am 6:1,4-6).

Traveling all morning, they arrived at Sychar at the sixth hour, that is, at noon. Jesus dismissed the disciples to fetch provisions. The sun, white-hot and blinding, was high in the sky. While townspeople were taking their sleep on shaded rooftops, Jesus, walking alone through the deserted afternoon, passed the amphitheater and stadium that Herod, who had married a Samaritan, had built. As at first when he had to pass through Samaria, now he had to pass through colonnaded streets. He approached the village well that was the reason why he had to pass this way.

Arriving at the well he saw a woman who was bent over her chore. One would wonder why she had chosen to come at noon. One would wonder why she, too, was not on the rooftop, taking sleep and shade from this hot and blinding Samaritan hour.

Arriving at the well, Jesus considered her carefully. Her face, layered in veils, did not reveal its features. Her large hands were seen and they were wrinkled. In fact, the shape of her whole figure showed unmistakably the fatigue and labor of the years. He had never seen his mother, aunts or cousins wear their hair the way hers was worn. If he had had a mother, aunts or cousins from Athens he would have. It was kept by ivory combs.

She had come to the well at the sixth hour when no one else would be there. She was no longer able to abide the morning slander of the women and no longer willing to endure their defamation. Looking at her Jesus saw there a burden heavier than that which any wooden yoke had to bear. This burden not only calloused her spine, but weighed down her spirit.

They stood looking at one another. Who, she thought, was this man? She wondered what would happen next. Jesus, however, knew what would happen next, even as he realized from the first that he had to pass this way.

Though neither the Samaritan Moses nor the Judean Moses condoned the act, the Jew and the Samaritan would speak. For man and woman to speak in public, even if they were married, was not acceptable. For Jew and Samaritan first to lift eyes to one another and then to lift voices was flagrant and reprehensible. They would speak, for this is why he had to pass this way. Then, after they had lifted their eyes and voices to one another, they would lift their souls to one another. It was required of him. He spoke at last and asked for water.

"Woman," he said, not afraid that his Galilean tongue would identify him, "give me to drink."

"This is astonishing," she said. "You ask me for water to drink? You, a man and a Jew, ask me, a woman and a Samaritan for water to drink? You would place yourself in debt to me and bring against my own face a husband's bruising hand in anger?"

Though she could not know it, her concern was unfounded. For he was not like her, that is, he cared not to whom he placed himself in debt. She did not know that he had to pass through Samaria. She did not know that this journey and this request of his was in fulfillment of the will of the Most High. She could not know. She knew his speaking and his request as forwardness only, merely as much effrontery. This was worse than even the severe morning cruelty she endured.

How inconsiderate and importune it was. Consider the jeopardy in which it placed her. For a woman even to speak with a man in public would be cause enough for punishment. When her husband heard of this, and hear of it he was certain to, it would make no difference if he learned that it was the man and not she who had initiated the conversation. It would be reason for another beating from a husband who had sent a wife only to fetch water and not to flirt. In addition, for a Samaritan like her to speak to a Jew like him would surely arouse the anger of the rabbi, who never lost the opportunity to renew fires of hatred between these two separated provinces. Remember John Hyrcanus in the time of the Maccabeans. He burned the temple of the Samaritans. Its foundation and ruins stood on Gerizim as reminder of a debt that waited for settlement.

"Woman," Jesus said, speaking neither of the debt nor of the largess of the Most High. "If only you knew all that the Most High our Father gives and who it is that even now asks of you for water to drink, you would have been prompt to ask and he would have given you living water."

"Sir," she answered, "remember the season. The wadi is dry. Little children dance on its stones. There is no living water now in any of Sychar. Or, sir, are you as great as you are bold? Are you greater than father Jacob who gave this spring and land for which he paid one hundred pieces silver, to son Joseph? How can you, sir, give me water? You have no bucket."

"Woman," he said, "you come here daily and fetch water, only to have your thirst return. The one who drinks of the water that I give will never thirst again."

Now she laughed. "Sir," she said, "it would be fine if anyone, Samaritan or Judean, could do that, for who wants this drudgery?"

Then, willing to take the risk, she dropped her bucket over the side and when it had filled with water, she returned it by gathering the rope in her hands. Then this woman presented water to the Savior of all; Jew and Samaritan, no difference, man and woman, no difference, the pure and the blemished, no difference. Having taken this water first to his lips, he poured the gift of Jacob's well conservatively, then lavishly over beard and head until it fell heedlessly to a thirsty earth. It was the dry season.

Refreshed now, Jesus said, "As you say, this spring and well was father Joseph's. He was sold by brothers as a slave to Egypt. Caravans still pass upon Samaritan roads, looking for a brother's treachery and for water. I have come to Joseph's spring and land to recall his memory."

"Sir," she answered, "do you mean that to this day Judea and Samaria are angry brothers? Is that why you say that you have come 'to recall his memory'?"

Jesus answered this by saying, "Woman, go and bring your husband, that he might drink this water here with us and be refreshed."

His request troubled her. She should have known earlier. Hadn't she sensed there was something troubling and inviting about him from the start? There was something about the eyes, the imploring words, the bravery and even about his presence in Samaria. There was something troubling, too, about his knowledge of men and women. By remaining at this well and by standing there with him, she would be the next object of his knowledge. It was one thing to have been willing to lift her face and her voice to him. Could she now go one moment more without lifting soul to him as well? The bucket, yes, that could be lifted, the eyes and voice, yes, they could be lifted. Not the soul — for it was too weighted with pain. So she fought his request.

Though it was a lie to say it, she answered, "Sir, I have no husband." The woman must not be judged for this, for though it was a lie, it was an excusable one. She had been hurt so and needed some ground on which to stand. It was justice for her to select the ground on which to rest a defense. That is why she told this lie. Did anyone have a right to require that she incriminate herself as he was asking? She saw it as a way of clearing space.

The answer registered with him as a lie and as an unnecessary one. He who understood every aggrieved heart would stop her now. For he himself would be her defense. She would not need, however licitly or illicitly, to clear ground.

"Yes, woman, you have spoken correctly," he said. "You

have no husband. The truth is that five have shared your nights. The one who does so now is not your husband. You are no different than this nation."

Now the lie was uncovered. What would she do next? She changed the subject. "Sir," she said, "I see you are a prophet. You and all in Judea and Galilee insist that it is only in Jerusalem that the Most High can be approached by offering and sacrifice. We claim that this place is preferred and that it is only on this mountain, Gerizim, that the Most High accepts tribute."

"Woman," Jesus answered, "Amen! Amen! I say to you, the day dawns when neither on this mountain nor in Jerusalem, on neither mountain, will the Most High our Father be honored. Then they who worship will worship in Spirit and in truth. I tell you that from now, only the Spirit is preferred and neither Gerizim nor Zion."

"Sir," she answered, "tell me who is the Messiah, that I might have the truth. Tell me of this Spirit, that I might worship. Tell me, sir."

"Woman," said Jesus, "the one who speaks to you, the one who had to pass this way, the one who asks you for water, he is the one whom you seek, for he is Spirit and truth, for he is all worship of the Most High our Father."

As water refreshes, so now did his words relieve shame and console her embittered soul. Thus that day not only her thirst but also her heart, which had been dry and cracked as the wadi, was healed and readied for service in the kingdom. Knowing this at last she made bold to lift her soul unto him.

"You know me, sir," she said. "How is it that you know me? You search me through with your eyes. Then with your mercy you lift my soul. How is it that you know me?" But he would not answer this, for he had already revealed enough about his knowledge.

Then, with all haste she rushed to those whose voices and glances she had tried so to avoid. She went to the very ones who had grieved her by their judgments. She said to them, "Hurry and see the one who told me all that I ever did and told me all that I ever suffered and then lifted my soul which had been so weighed with burden and sorrow." Up and down the streets she ran, climbing and descending outdoor stairs, shaking the townspeople from their sleep and shade with her excitement and her message; telling them of all that had occurred at the well.

"See the one," she cried, "who makes peace at last between Judea and Samaria and who levels both of our mountains. He raises a new mountain, the mountain of Spirit and of truth. Blessed be the Most High," she said; "who makes us to worship in Spirit and in truth."

The people were awakened that day and rushed to the well. They left their rooms whose fine paneling was inlaid with ivory. Leaping quickly from rooftop to rooftop, they did not even take time to descend to the colonnaded streets. In their tunics, cream in color, they made it all look like a field turned white.

One said, "Can it be ancestor Joseph, returned to drink from the spring which father Jacob gave and from which he drank, with sons and cattle?"

Another agreed, "It is Joseph, having mercy upon his brothers again; not with grain, but now with water. It is Joseph walking again among his tribes Ephraim and Manasseh."

As it is when the almond tree with white blossoms is the first to bloom, then, for Jesus, too, it was like the early awakening of the spring. Rising from their sleep on the rooftops they made, from his vantage, the whole earth look like so much spring, like so much Spirit and so much truth. Yes, this is why he had to pass this way, to urge forth this spring. He remained watching this different kind of spring as her cries aroused the village.

The disciples, having gone forth to secure provisions, were now returning. They discovered Jesus watching the sight of the townspeople hurrying to the well, anxious to discover for themselves what the woman was announcing. Now the townspeople all proclaimed it freely, one to the other. "It is father Joseph among us again."

Then the disciples stopped looking at the fields and at the white spring. Unlike Jesus they were not considering the almond tree that blossoms first and white. Thinking only of their own hunger, they said to him, "Rabbi, have you eaten?"

They never understood anything. This was because they had not the Spirit; not as yet, that is.

"Yes, I have eaten," Jesus said.

Whispering, they passed the explanation among themselves, "Someone has arrived with provisions."

"No," he corrected them. "I have food of which you know not. My food is to do the will of the one who sent me."

But again, not having understood about the tunics, the rooftops or the almond tree that blooms, how could they have understood this? They had not even understood why he had to pass through Samaria on his way to Galilee. Simon had recommended footpaths along the valley Jordan. Only Andrew had sensed the urgency. If they had not understood why he had to pass this way, could they ever understand that he had not eaten or, more importantly, that there was to be one more noon and one more thirst for him? For brothers again were to break faith with a father's son. At the noon that was still to come, Jesus would cry out in thirst for father Joseph's water for one final time.

For a long time now he was silent. Then his finger pointed in the direction of the townspeople. Breaking his silence, he answered the disciples, "See the fields. They are already white with harvest."

10

A Rich Young Man Goes Away Sad

Jesus looked at him and said, "How hard it is for those who have riches to make their way into the kingdom of God! Yes, it is easier for a camel to pass through the eye of a needle than for someone rich to enter the kingdom of God."

(Luke 18:24-27)

Those who did not know him well would never have imagined that the day would come when the rich young man would be sent on his way by Jesus. Yes, who would have understood why he, with such ability and charm, would not have been allowed to continue to travel in the company of Jesus? But then these were the same who would have thought that the rich young man would have understood the importance of gladness in Israel. That explains why they were surprised that on one night a year before he had not rejoiced.

That night, having presided all through an arduous day over slaves in the vineyards of his father, all imperiousness and energy, he returned to hear music of gladness coming forth from the house. Those who knew him would not have been surprised; no, not on that one night, nor on the day one year later when he was dismissed from the company by Jesus.

Returning home now, the rich young man admitted how similar he and his father were. In this way the wisdom of the rabbinate was indisputable: the apple falls not far from the tree. On the one hand, like father, the rich young man had not been infected with the usual selfishness of the wealthy. On the other, like father, the rich young man had developed a fine way of deploying generosity, that is, of using it to maintain the affections of others. In other words, the rich young man came with every gift he offered. He was attached to every favor he urged upon you. He was interest paid on every loan he provided. Indeed, with every forkful of lamb eaten while reclining at table, you were required to digest him as well.

Yet his was such flawless style that no one had an idea. He had long since mastered the art of at one moment being reserved enough to draw your curiosity, and then, at the next, being expressive enough to claim your affection. He was master of all charm. Increased familiarity with him only intensified the trance. For example, you discovered that what he both did and said was entirely appropriate. The right answer and the correct explanation was his. A naturalness about the flow of his words made one think that he had not plotted the direction of every word.

With what effect the rich young man worked a crowd and how he maintained their loyalties. So liked was he that very few, those who knew him were too few, were aware of how infectious was his charm. Others, even those older or more experienced than he, felt confident in his presence and took well to being instructed by the instruction for living that issued forth from him. Continually those to whom he was so attractive surrounded him. Some would ape the fashions and expressions of the rich young man.

How often his father had been praised: "Your eldest! What breeding! What intelligence! What charm is his!" The father was wiser than this flattery. Observing his son's minions, the father drew his own conclusions. After all, the rich young man was his son and the apple falls not far from the tree.

The rich young man was flawed. It was neither in the charm nor in the poise. It was neither in the tact nor in the discretion. They were flawless. Here was his flaw: though the rich young man could love, he could not much be loved. And his charm was wholly channeled to prevent others from giving to him. This is what the father first knew and what later, on the day of excommunication, Jesus would reveal that he too had come to know.

If you were chosen by the rich young man to be his friend, then, believe this, our brother Cain was no more marked than you were. For all so selected, there was no end of his kindness or of his requirement that you accept his favor. On your birthday, he would plan a banquet in your honor. May the Most High come to the aid of any who would not accept the invitation. His attention to detail was extreme. It was a fact that no cook could work long for him. Inevitably he would seize spoon and knife from the cook as if he were mighty Caesar himself marching into battle's fray to relieve the highest general of the empire of the white cape of command.

As time had gone on, the need of the rich young man to give became unlimited. Though still in the employ of his father, he yearned not for wife and sons, not for fruitful vineyards, not for sacks of gold, but instead for his own table where he, too, could reign indomitably, as did his father.

Yes, the rich young man discovered it harder and more difficult to be a son in the home of his father. He resented his father's presidency at table. In fact, to recline there lowered his spirits. Not that he did not love his father, but rather that it reminded him of what he desired for himself. More than anything he needed to provide. If there were a table at which to recline, he needed to be the one to recline at the head of it and then position all others. He needed to be the one to announce the vintage, to praise the lamb and bless the Most High, and later to be credited for generosity displayed in the formulation of the guest list.

This, he now admitted, had been the substance of his problem that final night at home. Now it was a year later and he had been excommunicated from the company by Jesus. Returning to the home of his father, he saw the truth of it clearly.

The night a year ago had been the night his slothful and impious younger brother had returned from a time of revelry that had nearly bankrupted the estate. Wholly impoverished, his brother had left a gentile city famished and wearing robes that were not clothes at all, for they were torn and sorry rags. As for scent, the only scent recognized at the time of his brother's homecoming was the putrid smell of swine that this pathetic one had tended when he could no longer afford to maintain even appearances.

On the night a year ago it was dark by the time the steed of the rich young man and the train of slaves had returned to the main compound of the estate. Approaching, they heard sounds of rejoicing and wondered what these could mean. Over the low roofs of his father's house they saw the glow of lamps illuminating the courtyard and in the air they smelled the aroma of cooking bread and roasting lamb. One servant rushed to greet him.

"What goes on here? Why the light and the aromas in the air?" the rich young man asked as the servant advanced.

"Your brother is returned," the astonishing answer cut through the darkness of the night, "and your father has killed the fatted calf."

His anger was immediate. "Let them dance and drink until the next moon," the rich young man cursed.

Now, with one year and with the company of Jesus behind him, and returning to the home of his father, the rich young man accepted what it was that had really bothered him about his brother's return. It was not his brother's squandering of family wealth, or the pleasures he had taken in the company of whores. It was not the putrid smell of swine on him or even the sorrow that pierced his father's heart. No, it was something more subtle. It was the fact that his brother had not first sought his support.

Had he come to him, instead of to his father, and pleaded for him to intercede on his behalf, then it would have been all different. That would have given him the opportunity to be his

110

brother's counselor before his father. Then, having persuaded, it would have been the privilege of the elder brother to call for the rejoicing and to have the enduring appreciation of his brother.

No, the rich young man would not agree, even when his father came to him to plead in the name of the Most High that he enter into the rejoicing. Raising his voice, he invoked Moses, even though Moses was not the issue. "What of the law of the Most High, my father?"

For the voice of son to be raised against father was something unheard of in Israel, and even more of an abomination in a faithful household like theirs. That is some measure of how much had been lost that night between father and son.

The fury of the rich young man continued to rage: "You taught us to reverence and obey the law. In that law it is written that we honor father and mother. My brother has sinned against that law in his gentile cities, with his gentile women, and with the gentile swine which he, in his loneliness, found to be his only friends. After he has broken faith against your name and against the Most High, you welcome him as if he were our father Samuel returning to judge the tribes."

Then came final words which were the worst because they were the most untrue. The rich young man said, "You have never given me and my friends as little as the side of a kid with which to celebrate."

No, that was not the truth. Now, one year later and an excommunicate, the rich young man could admit that truth that night had been elsewhere than in his words about the cut of meat. Though at the time it would not have been possible for the rich young man to admit, there was more honesty that night in the imploring breath of the younger son, reeking stench though it was, than in his sweet breath.

That night one year ago the rich young man told his father that the time had arrived for him to depart the estate and devote himself to furthering family business in cities and towns. Though it was the loss of another son, to this the father agreed and on the next day the rich young man departed to begin a new life away from the table and away from the mercies of his father. For that world was the father's world, not his.

Ironic and how droll it was that now one year later, the rich young man was returning. His homecoming would be of a different sort than had been his brother's. The funds of the rich young man were in place; in fact, he had acquired many new accounts for his father's wines. His robes were not torn. No, the garments of the rich young man were new and handsome robes, sewn in foreign cities. Their threads were silver and scarlet.

When it came to scents, his were not the scents of gentiles or of swine. His were the most esoteric of scents known in Judea. For scent, too, he was partial to what came from other places. His choice was found only at one booth in the temple market, a booth where, though many came to inhale and admire the workers in their handsome finery, few could afford to buy. Reasoning that it was best to use one only and none other, the rich young man always used the same oil. In this way, he thought, others would acquire knowledge of his scent. They would remain in his possession in this olfactory fashion. Of this, once, while under the influence of wine, he explained to a friend, "The Most High has given us many faculties. It pleases the Most High that we make the most of this one."

He did not use it as a way of pleasing the Most High. Rather, he used it to impose, even to importune himself on others whom he imagined later, remembering his scent; remembering that which would bring him and no one else to mind.

Returning now one year later and in a state of excommunication, his steed carried him along the road which led to his father's house. He thought of its rooftop.

It was as fine a rooftop as any in Israel. Upon its floor were inlaid marble stones. Around its ledge were statues of the Judges of Israel which had been carved from cedar. Years before, as a youth, he had commissioned a famous sculptor in Jerusalem to produce these as a gift for his father. He required, at first much to the surprise of the sculptor and later to the surprise of all who admired them, that the judge Deborah be included.

It was on that rooftop that the family met as Friday's departing sun submitted to dusk and sabbath. The rich young man remembered the glow of candlelight, the breeze that in itself was all consolation, and the light from other families' candles that illuminated their rooftops, making the whole village a sea of light and a sea of fidelity to the prescriptions of father Moses who had ordered sabbath observance.

How his father had taught both sons to obey father Moses and to reverence every prescription of the law; yet, how gentle was the heart of this man. For example, the rich young man recalled how even though theirs was as fine a rooftop as any, he and his brother had been taught to eschew pride. Their father had emphasized that even the rooftops of the poor were to be regarded with highest reverence. On those rooftops, no less than on theirs, the pious father taught, the Most High visits his people to take sabbath rest and to enjoy the breeze that in itself is all consolation.

Always during supper on sabbath, the father would instruct the sons on the wisdom of the law. Then he would bless the Most High for the prescribed rest that permitted the halt of all work and worry for this one day so that instruction in Moses could proceed in Israel.

The father, as was his appointed duty and his joy, urged his sons to ask questions. One night, while but a small youth, the rich young man asked the father if the Most High was a God gracious or severe.

The father answered, "My son, first consider how it is of a father's nature to show mercy toward his own sons. For example, would a father in Israel give a son a stone if he had been asked for bread, or give a son a snake if he had been asked for fish? Then realize that if we, with all our sins, know how to give righteousness and mercy to our sons, how much more will our heavenly Father give the Holy Spirit to those who ask? That is how gracious is the Most High."

What devastation can the flight of a son, fed all through life on instruction and mercy, bring upon rooftops! For during the time of the absence of the brother of the rich young man this rooftop no longer was the privileged place for instruction of sons and for blessing of the Most High as rooftops were

113

intended to be for Israel. No, it had become his father's place
of vigil. He was seen there at the first light of dawn, almost as
if he were addressing the statues of the judges, pleading for
their appearance; and, if not for that, for at least a share of
their equanimity in trial. He was observed there again during
the afternoon when anyone with sense used rooftops for sleep
and not for weeping and he was seen pacing upon the rooftop
again as the last light parted earth and the moon rose to share
his lonely vigil.

Asked why he spent all his time there the father would
deflect the truth. "It is to watch the fields and the vineyards
below," he would claim.

No, it was to watch the road that led to this place of vines,
to this home of an upright father who feared the Most High
and who had raised his sons in righteousness and mercy. For
what father in Israel provides stone when bread is required?
For what father in Israel offers a snake when it is fish that is
required? No. The reason for the vigil was to watch the road
for sight again of the one who had been lost.

Upon leaving the home of his father, the rich young man
traveled throughout the cities of Galilee and Judea. Though the
days were filled with a whirl of activity and enterprise, the
nights were another thing. They were loss and loneliness for
the rich young man. Since his charm and his poise were intact,
there were new friends and acquaintances in abundance.
These he regaled in inns and during dining as was his custom
and indeed his need; but, none of it satisfied. They could not
relieve that which had begun to burden him.

He found that of all things, he missed the rooftop and the
sabbath. He yearned to gaze again upon the faces of the
Judges of Israel. Now he, like his father, did yearn for their
equanimity in trial. He wished to know again the breeze that
was all consolation. He longed for the way his father blessed
the Most High as the Most High is only blessed in family, at
table, and by a father who is an upright man, author of sons in
Israel, and teacher of righteousness and mercy; and, finally as
the Most High is blessed only on sabbath. O! blessed sabbath.

That loneliness of soul and that homesickness for rooftop
and for sabbath led him, while staying in Bethany, to a certain

one named John who was causing a stir and commotion along the banks of the River Jordan. Though edifying to those on the shore, this one's preaching was consternation in the palace of Herod Antipas, adulterer and prince.

During the days the rich young man ventured forth to the River Jordan to hear. Who could say why the rich young man who had all the scent and robes one could desire, who had wealth and now even independence, and who had presidency over any congress for dinner, would venture forth to the River Jordan to hear another? But then, think of nights and how difficult they had become for him.

One day the rich young man stood next to one like unto himself in attractiveness, though not in either robes or scents. They both stood on the shoreline of the sea, and together heard John announce the winnowing fan. At the end of the day, the other whose name was Jesus, offered the rich young man bread from his belt to eat. After eating, the rich young man insisted that they depart together to an inn for dinner and for talk about what they had heard.

The two discovered that they had much in common. Day after day they went to hear John. In the afternoon Jesus offered the rich young man bread. Always the rich young man prevailed upon Jesus to return to the inn with him to dine and to speak more. While he was teaching Jesus to enjoy the inn with its baths and the opportunities of its table, Jesus was teaching the rich young man to understand more deeply the words of John and the nearness of the kingdom.

One cloudless day John called out for baptism. Like Jesus, the rich young man had heard John's cry and had been moved by it; but, unlike Jesus, the rich young man would not take off his cloak and submit to being washed. He was reluctant to impart to the waters of the Jordan the sweet, lingering, evocative scent, the scent that evoked him and not another. For what would life be like if he went into the Jordan with the scent, with the scent that was memorable for its fats and fragrance, which was intended to, and did, evoke the memory of him?

Jesus told him to believe in the Holy Spirit. "If it be the will of the Most High our Father," Jesus said, "baptism will be like the receiving of an answer to a question which no one else can answer. It might be like the hearing of a voice, a sound, or perhaps a thundering acclamation of words and volume from this cloudless sky."

To this the rich young man answered soberly, "Perhaps there will be only silence."

"Then," said Jesus, "Blessed be the Most High our Father for silence." Jesus would seek baptism and either its acclamation or its silence. The rich young man remained upon the shore.

Unlike the rest, when Jesus came to John, the baptist bent to whisper in his ear for a moment. Then, and this seemed odd, Jesus took the hand of John, as if he was responding to resistance, and set John's hand upon his own head. For one moment the sun seemed brighter in the eyes of the rich young man. This he dismissed as merely the movement of clouds that in their passage had momentarily uncovered the sun.

From then on, the rich young man traveled in what became the growing company of Jesus. During the day he listened to the words of Jesus and in the evenings, as Jesus sometimes permitted, the rich young man provided meals and inns for Jesus and the company. On the occasions this occurred, as was his wont, the rich young man presided.

As the company continued to increase in size, the rich young man experienced a certain apprehension, for he understood Jesus and had a sense for all that was in jeopardy by his association with him. In jeopardy were not inns and dinners. It was not the fancying of himself in his embroidered robe, or in joyous pastels. Neither was it the scent. No, it was not the thought that these would have to go. Something that he could not yet name, something deeper and more substantial was in jeopardy, and that is why he maintained himself with independence.

Jesus came to love the rich young man greatly. Jesus would later remember the moment when first he had come to realize this. It was the day when someone from the crowd asked Jesus if any one of the company — this was at first a preposterous question — if any one had given of the Spirit to others in the company.

Now though the question had been addressed to Jesus, to

the surprise of all, the rich young man answered it. Never had any one of the company presumed to answer a question addressed to Jesus; but, on this day, the rich young man, the one who remained apprehensive, the one of all knowledge and experience when it came to inns and menus and scents, provided the answer.

He said, "If one, if only one of us, has given of the Holy Spirit to another, to just one other, it is the same as if that one had given of the Holy Spirit to the entire company."

Jesus approved of the answer of the rich young man. No, Jesus did not smile because the rich young man was paying for the wine that evening. Rather, Jesus delighted in the sagacity of the answer. Of its unorthodoxy, too, and of the unexpectedness of its vision, Jesus approved. From then Jesus understood how deeply he loved him.

In this answer Jesus recognized the rich young man's defense for his continued presence within the company, however hedged and remote apprehension made it. It was as if the rich young man was saying that he should be allowed to continue if for not one other reason, because he had given of the Holy Spirit to one, and, by so doing, had given of the Holy Spirit to the whole company, for that is how it is with the Spirit.

That Jesus understood what was meant by the rich young man's answer was no surprise, for the two understood one another. When it came to this particular answer, Jesus did not miss the point that the rich young man had made. From then on, Jesus realized with what deep love he cared for the rich young man, who had seen so clearly what Jesus was always reiterating, the Spirit was one and the same.

That event composed in the mind of Jesus a portrait of the rich young man as one who did not live on the borrowed assertions of others. For the answer of the rich young man was not one more of the rented answers that Pharisees pumped out in every direction, without ever having had a thought of their own. The law they preached had not wisdom enough to inspire you in what to do. Its only authority was to instruct you in what not to do. Jesus recalled the sabbath teacher the rich young man had remembered from his father. The law gave stone when bread was required. The law gave a snake when it was fish that was required. The law was the personification of sameness.

Having been born to the letter of that law and never reborn to its spirit, the Pharisees relied on answers at which not one of them had ever arrived, largely because not one of them had ever had to help bear the burdens of another. For that matter, who among them had ever spoken about the Spirit? The rich young man could speak of the Spirit. That he had shown. Such ability always requires a certain unorthodoxy. This Jesus knew and indeed loved in the rich young man.

Like Jesus, the rich young man could not do with sameness. It was in this they were alike and it was for this reason that they understood one another. That is why the rich young man preferred imported goods and the statue of Deborah, the Judge of Israel, over all the rest. It was the reason why Jesus preferred the Spirit, that one and same Spirit, before the law. It was this quality that first had impressed Jesus about the rich young man and had first made Jesus set hope in the rich young man's presence in the company.

Jesus admitted that the rich young man would never be Simon. No, he could never be the leader of others, precisely because he was made so tired by sameness. He could never be bothered with the day to day. Best assign that to the Simons of the company, Jesus thought. Simon was good at mending nets and mending alliances. When it came to speaking about the Spirit, one would have to wait a long period of time before Simon would speak to say something worth remembering.

If this was the moment Jesus realized his love for the rich young man, it was also the moment when he realized that separation between the two was inevitable. Though Jesus had the sense that the rich young man was apt for unique service in the company, it became equally apparent that the rich young man would have to decide. Two events had led Jesus to that conclusion.

On the first occasion, a poor person had given Judas a gift of money and Jesus had directed that Judas provide from this, humble though it was, for the night's meal and lodging. Upon learning of the smallness of the sum, the rich young man was disappointed, for he had looked forward to comfortable accommodations that night. At the inn, he intervened and ordered a better entree and acquired finer rooms. From his own purse he paid the balance. The poor person, benefactor of the gift, knew what lamb and inns cost and was made to feel that his gift had been inadequate.

At another time the company had returned to the same village in Galilee where weeks before they had enjoyed the hospitality of a synagogue. Now the place had been a poor nothing, but the rabbi and his pious assembly of Israel had great heart. The Spirit had made them rejoice to give from their need to Jesus and to the company. Now Jesus and the company had returned to the place and were suprised to discover that the synagogue was undergoing an extensive building project. At the end of their earlier visit, and unknown to Jesus, the rich young man had provided the rabbi funds for the addition of extra rooms and a large kitchen. The rich young man, so uncomfortable with receiving and so fond of giving had again deprived poor ones who were rich in the Spirit of the greatest joy there is to be had in the kingdom; that is, the joy of giving to others even when your own need remains great. Jesus could not abide these injustices. He would spend the night in prayer.

The next morning, Jesus returned to the company and selecting 12 of them, breathed upon their heads. But he did not breathe upon the head of the rich young man.

The rich young man was disappointed, for who among the company had supported the campaign as ardently as he? And who in the company had ever answered with insight which Jesus approved, a question from the crowd?

With this, the day had come for Jesus to tell him at last to set aside his embroidery and free himself of the aromatic butters and of the inns, and more importantly to lay down the giving; and, then to follow him and the company into a new way of living. If this the rich young man could not do, then, Jesus decided, deep love or no deep love, the day had arrived to excommunicate the rich young man from the company.

It was the day that Jesus, upon naming the twelve, brought them into the center of the company and breathed upon their heads. Later that day the rich young man initiated the conversation: "You did not breathe upon my head. Why was not mine one of the names the Spirit whispered to you last night while you prayed?" he asked of Jesus. "It is my wealth. Is it not? Am I not generous with my wealth and am I not ready to place it all at the disposition of the campaign?"

"It is not your wealth. It is that you are not ready yet," Jesus said, "for the cup that is to be drunk in the kingdom."

"Offer me that cup now. Offer me that cup this morning, so that I might take it to my lips and drink deeply of it. Offer me that cup now so that the angel might come tonight and whisper my name to you. So that then you might breathe upon my head as breathe you did upon the heads of Simon and of John, upon the heads of James and of Philip, upon the heads of Bartholomew and of Judas and the rest."

"You who are glib and whose words are always smooth, your purse has betrayed you," Jesus answered. "You use your purse for more than the purchase of scent and of supper, for more than rooms in which to sleep and litters upon which to be carried forth. You use your purse to buy freedom from what in your mind is the only impoverishment, the impoverishment of being in debt to another."

"If this is so, then tell the Spirit what poor choices have been made." No, the rich young man would not hear the truth. "For those upon whom you breathed this morning are far from perfect. Simon, for example, has the complexity of the spoon."

Jesus did not need to be informed of this analogy, for he knew well about Simon's kinship with the spoon. In some ways, the rich young man was correct. There is always some measure of truth in what people say. Yes, he was different than the rest. Jesus had not forgotten either the insight shown in the answer about the Holy Spirit or of the rich young man's boredom, all yawns and weariness it was, with sameness. Neither had he forgotten the rich young man's potential to contribute to the company.

There was something else that Jesus would not let the rich young man forget. "The others have in an easy abundance the one thing required for life in the kingdom, and it is the one thing you lack."

"What is that?" asked the rich young man.

"It is the peace that comes from receiving. Theirs is the ability to stand in debt, one to the other, and all of them to me, and through me to the Most High our Father. You who are always giving have never permitted yourself to receive."

The rich young man defended himself. "I want to do for others. What is wrong or grievous about that?"

Jesus tested him with a question. "Answer this one question correctly and I will breathe upon you and you will be numbered among the company. On what occasions is it better to receive rather than give?"

The rich young man answered swiftly, "On some occasions it is better to receive than to give."

That was the wrong answer, precisely the wrong answer. For Jesus, there was only one answer, and it was the answer that all of the twelve, for all their faults, and yes, even Simon who was as simple as the spoon, could answer. This was the correct answer: on all occasions it is better to receive than to give just as on all occasions it is better that power over one's life be relinquished; not on some as the rich man had answered, but on all. In this is the Holy Spirit.

The Pharisees liked wealth. Having observed what this had done to their spirit, Jesus had come not to like wealth because it prevented interdependence. On this day, and for this reason, this 13th apostle would be excommunicated by Jesus; neither for his scent nor for his familiarity with the inns, neither for his steed nor for embroidery, nor for his preference for the uncommon. In spite of the fact that in all things he had signature, it was for his decision to use wealth so that he need not depend on any other person. That is why the Spirit had not whispered his name to Jesus.

The way of the rich young man was not of the Holy Spirit because there was never anything that he had received for which he had not paid. It was the same with the Holy Spirit. Though the rich young man had given of the Holy Spirit, he would not allow Jesus to give to him of the same Holy Spirit in return. That is what Jesus sought to do for him and for the rest of the company. The rich young man needed to lay aside the need to give and his compulsion to repay and, indeed, over-compensate, after he had received. In this Jesus was seeking to give to the rich young man of the one and same Holy Spirit.

That Spirit was not to be received. The gift which the rich young man was able to give was the one gift he was too flawed to receive. This was the same flaw that prevented the rich young man from sharing in the joy that night one year before when he returned from the fields to see light over his father's courtyard. It was the same flaw that prevented him from giving the scent of his arms and hair to the Jordan. Now this would demand that Jesus, for all the love he shared with the rich young man, require that he decide.

The rich young man and Jesus understood one another. Even in their parting they showed their love. "Sometimes you are raised up by the Spirit," the rich young man said as he was making ready to leave, "and sometimes the Spirit falls upon you."

To this Jesus answered, "And at still other times, we simply say that the Spirit is within; that is, that the one and same Spirit is within our souls."

The rich young man said, "May the Holy Spirit fall anew upon the tribes and may the Holy Spirit raise up the company of the Christ."

Jesus added, "May the Spirit abide within all those who upon the rooftops of Israel seek the breeze that is in itself all consolation and seek the praise of the Most High our Father."

With final words about the one and the same Spirit the rich young man parted the company. Jesus who loved the rich young man and who saw sadness line his face as he left, would come to regard this as the day of greatest sorrow in the kingdom.

The steed carrying the rich young man to the house of his father now drew close to its destination. As his beast navigated the final turn in the road, the house composed itself in his view. The eyes of this elder son were raised to the rooftop of his father's house, an upright father who feared the Most High and who had raised sons for Israel in righteousness and mercy. It was the finest rooftop in all of Israel. Along its ledge was a line of statues carved from cedar. They were of our fathers and, yes, of our mother, the Judges of Israel.

11

The Widow Who Gave Everything

A poor widow came and put in two small coins, the equivalent of a penny.
(Mark 12:42)

Her husband had always complained when he noticed her extravagance in giving things away. But, she insisted, such readiness was a qualification for living. About this, at least, she was confident, and he had never argued that she wasn't. "Anyway," she defended the generosity, "the Most High has cut short the time. What need is there to have extra on hand?" Perhaps it was precisely this extravagance that had seen her through great reversals.

They had a first-born whom they loved. Yet as he grew, his complaints about Rome were more and more bitter. Having been touched by the revolutionary spirit, he had left their house, for they had been unable to reason with him. He joined the forces of the Zealots. Next his parents heard that he had been part of a minor rebellion somewhere.

125

After a woefully mismatched skirmish with some imperial legionnaires who had been quartered in the village, he had been captured. A centurion had ordered him carried off to slavery for the empire. Where he had been taken, mother and father were not told. The husband readily admitted that she coped with the loss with more grace than he. At this moment of suffering she had insisted that she was certain, more than ever, that the Most High had cut short the time.

After her husband died she recalled their betrothal. At the time a contract had been signed. Yes, she remembered that. For a fee, a Pharisee from the next village came when summoned. Upon arriving he conducted the prenuptial questionnaire that conformed to canons prescribed for all synagogues in this district wherein both land and children were fertile.

In the Pharisee's bag was the standard contract. As in all such contracts was the promise requiring that a certain part of the dowry be retained by the wife against the day she should become a widow. However, by the time he died, this dowry, which hadn't been substantial even at the start, had long since been spent. She recalled clearly the circumstances during which her entitlement had been surrendered.

One year Caesar's legions needed revenue so his infantry could be equipped with tools and shields. That year, too, Herod, the great builder, had wanted an aqueduct so water could push back the desert and he could have new fields with which to award supporters. That year the high priest needed a new curtain for the Holy of Holies, so that on the feast of Atonement he would not have to look again at the same embroidery as the previous year. So the assessment for tax was raised sharply.

In one last effort to save their fertile property on the Plain of Esdraelon, she presented her husband with the part of the dowry that according to the justice of father Moses and the law was hers and not his, however futile were the circumstances. The husband had not required of the wife that she present him with this. An oath before father Moses had been sealed by the notarizing Pharisee which reserved it for her against the day that she should become a widow. She gave it all now to her husband. Though he hesitated at her characteristic extravagance, she was unhesitating. "Nothing new in your objection," she said, "it is easier to give than receive." She would claim no virtue for her generosity. Of her, to a friend he said, "What great soul she has." She told him not to make too much either of it or of her soul. The money was given to the collector. Perhaps they would survive.

Though this was a great act of a great soul, still it was not enough. The collector, sympathetic to Herod but not to them, arrived and confiscated their farm. He did it all with none of the ceremony that the Pharisee from the next town had shown when he had come to administer for father Moses and for the fee, the rites of betrothal. Cruel Herod amalgamated what had been theirs with the many other modest ancestral farms upon which he also had been able to foreclose. It had been a good year for army equipment, for desert aqueducts and for temple curtains. It had not been such for this wife and husband.

That was the end of their lands, and, for husband, though not for wife, the end of all hope as well. Now a beaten and humiliated man, the husband hired himself as an indentured laborer to work on the same property that had once been his to work as owner, as it had been the pride of his father and of fathers before him. To the wife, the husband came with the type of overwhelming sadness and loss that cannot be much comforted.

"All is lost," his lips whispered, moving over and over, often without sound, repeating the despair. "All is lost."

To give to him now was harder than in the past, for giving to him now required that she listen and be helpless. That is what he needed. For her, accustomed as she was to providing solutions and doing tasks, to be helpless was difficult. Still, she continued the effort. During the day, his hours were listless and wholly without peace.

In the evenings, while his head rested on her lap she stroked his face and kissed his hands and ears. At times, though not often, she spoke.

"Such an injustice. Such an injustice," she whispered on one such occasion to help him. These words, small indeed as they seemed to her, helped him. Yet in spite of her efforts which were as great as her soul, in spite of the kissing and the whispering, he remained joyless. "This is the one thing that never changes," she thought. "It is easier to give than receive."

At night the memory of it worsened. His rest was fitful and without sleep and often she felt his whole body leap to cry out on the mat on which they slept. "My husband," she said, "it is as it is written in the psalms, 'at night weeping enters in.' "

Throughout this period not once did she think of herself. His pain was so much more vast than hers that it claimed preeminence. Perhaps it was her salvation that she was humble about this strength. She was helpless to persuade. Reason could not convince him. However steep had been the taxes and however impossible to meet, still he felt that he had failed in sacred duty and that when tested he had come up short on honor. After all, was it not the essence of honor for the husband to provide? Was it not for husband to hold onto lands that had been his family's for generations? He mourned for himself. As time went on she watched the devastation become comprehensive. Through all, this great soul of a wife continued.

In their marriage, even after the loss of her son, and even in these reduced circumstances, she had never much worried for the wherewithal for life. All she had wanted was enough food and enough strength. For her, enough was enough. Who needed to think about wherewithal when you seemed to have enough?

Then one afternoon, men came to her house with news that threatened even that. Even before the first words tumbled forth from them, the look on their faces informed her of a situation whose gravity would test her extravagance. As they spoke she squeezed her eyes so tightly closed that first she saw only black and then only white. She panted for breath. Still all the squeezing and the panting would not make their message go away.

There had been fire in the granary, they said. The first wheat harvest at Pentecost had been an exceedingly large crop. Late summer crops promised to be an unusually bountiful harvest as well. For the owner who had been awarded these lands by Herod, enough was not enough. The silos were deemed not to be adequate. With a flourish he directed that they be dismantled and that more accommodating ones be constructed. The owner was inspecting her husband's work on this project when fire began. It spread through the piled harvest bales. Both owner and husband succumbed to smoke and flame.

The day at last had come, she thought, for them to stand before the judgment seat of the Most High. The day had come for her husband to be comforted and the injustice lifted. That is the way it was with the Most High, she knew. To the Most High neither bitterness nor greed made any difference, each were weighty things on the human soul. Before the judgment seat, the Most High would set these forth in kindness, in one last eternal kindness. It was the way of the Most High to be kind eternally. The rabbi always taught that through the flood the Most High had judged the earth with water, but the next time the Most High would act with fire. Could it be that now the Most High had cut short the time at last? It seemed.

Now she was a widow of Israel and for her the task was to set forth her own life for survival. More than anything, she wanted to do what she always did, that is, to carry on. So while her husband's friends in the village met each day in the synagogue to pray and shiver for this life that had ended by smoke and flame, and for some to envy that it was concluded, she moved from the place on the fertile plain, the place that had known such bereavement and traveled to Jerusalem.

In Israel, it was important to show reverence for widows. She could expect to receive the hospitality of kin because she was a widow and therefore it was required to make room for another. Without any balance left in her dowry, she could offer these kin no funds of her own. They would not expect any. About this she was not too pleased. Remember that she believed that it was easier to give than receive. She knew that her presence would be a strain for these kin who were poor, poor in means, even if they were rich in mercy to a widow.

Though their home could accommodate her, she was determined to contribute whenever possible, for their own finances were meager. Once when she was young and her eyes had been good, she embroidered. She was accomplished at it.

Tourists and pilgrims arrived in Jerusalem hoping to purchase such fine things. But her days of embroidering were at an end. Her vision had deteriorated. Her eyes, milky and cloudy in appearance, were not healthy. What she still could do was run a spinner. After the lambs had been sheared, there were always bales of raw wool for spinning. You did not need sharp eyesight for that. In this, too, she was frustrated for this was the wrong season for spinning. When she arrived in Jerusalem the lambs were still short of fleece, and thus she remained short of funds. She thought to herself that this was the time to be resourceful.

She decided to become a wailer. By day she loitered in the temple precincts. Though such loitering to hear news of death was a grim way to earn a living, she was resigned to it. Upon hearing of a death, she rushed to present herself at the home in widow's attire and recommended her services to the family. The bereaved, especially those who neither could nor would cry themselves, were always grateful for a din. Nothing dignified obsequies like a tumult; the now shaking, now hysterical, now contained, now concentrated pouring forth of tears and lament.

She became quite expert. At first sobbing for a fee did not come easily and her form was rather mechanical and overdone. Her wailing had the "forced" quality to it that no one prefers. In her own life, tears were one thing in which she had not much indulged. She showed improvement with the steady business that came her way.

At the beginning she had a method to induce tears. Once in the home and before the corpse she remembered the trials of her own life. On the one hand, her tears were artificial, since they were not specifically for the soul for whom she had been hired to raise a tumult. On the other hand, her tears were genuine, since she shed them for the suffering that was endemic to all living. So, in part, she shed them for the first-born who now was a slave somewhere, but where, she did not know. Of course, the weeping was for the husband whom she had lost because the silos were too small and larger ones needed to be built; and, certainly, they were for the owner, for whom enough was not enough.

To home after home she went in response to announce-
ments of death. She went to wail and raise a din. There were
women to whom death came after long and gruesome illnesses
during which they withered to nothing in weight. Or, it was
for one of the husbands of Jerusalem, a man vigorous and
strong, who had collapsed dead suddenly one day at the
bazaar. Or, it was for a young child, just three years and
talking, who developed a fever as hot as a furnace, and, like
her own husband, died in conflagration. She noted that both
to young and old, death came. To the well-heeled and the
impoverished, to Roman and Jew, to those in the honored
professions and those in despised trades, death came. For the
lepers, too, death came. She did not need to go and wail for
them, because the law proscribed contact with the leper even
after death. For them, she thought, tears were not in order,
since their death was an end of sorrow.

Slowly something occurred. She became more genuine at
her responsibilities. It was far more than the achievement of
more convincing style or of more thrilling performance. More
and more she felt the urgency of tears. The frequency of death
that she witnessed opened her eyes to this. While it was the
sense of time cut short returning again, it was now more
imperative. Why, she could not say for certain. She began to
believe that the Most High was cutting short the time in a
fashion that, in her naivete, she had never understood before.
This great soul believed that it needed to expand more and
more, as a way of witnessing to this ongoing act of the Most
High.

So many misunderstood, she began to realize. They were
waiting for the roof to fall from under them during afternoon
sleep, or, as she had been, expecting the end to be as dramatic
as a first-born and much beloved being carried off to slavery, or
a husband succumbing to smoke and flames in a granary. Now
she felt that in regard to judgment, she had expected the
wrong things. Judgment had come into the world. Yes, it was
at hand; but what sudden light, this salvation. The more
complete truth was that it was always at hand and accessible.
At least, so she felt. Still something seemed to be missing.

Yes, her soul increased. She found herself returning to the

131

homes even after the mourning was over and she had received her fee. She proved of great help to families. When she judged that it would be of assistance, she told her own tale of loss and bereavement. Often that proved to give courage. When she could, she would return to help a widower who had never learned to cook or carry water, or with coins she could spare for another widow who, unlike her, had no kin to help, or with toys to little children who had lost their mother or father. She returned with her joy and abandon, and her extravagance of spirit. Yes, more and more she was convinced, the time had been cut short. Her husband had been correct when he had said, "What great soul she has."

One day she went to a certain home to wail. It was unusually sad, for this was a young woman who had died suddenly on the day before her wedding was to occur. She had complained of a headache. While the family dismissed it as merely a case of nervousness, she told them that the pain was as intense as death. Then she fell into her father's arms. They dressed her in wedding robes. On her left arm, and close to her heart, like a phylactery, they tied the marriage contract. All sworn and signed, it was never to be fulfilled. Though in this home that day there were abundant tears, the widow lingered to contribute hers.

Someone reached the young man who was to be her husband. He rushed into the room and looked upon his bride, his eyes revealing an implosion of grief. Later, in describing his arrival, the widow would swear she had never seen such pain before. Now along with his, fresh tears from those who thought they had spent all their reservoir had flowed again in profligate rivers.

Then there was noise at the door. Another had arrived. Could anyone believe this? The hysterical father, so desperate by his pain, had persuaded some wonderworker to come. The widow regarded this all as so much grossness. Next the newly arrived man directed the mourners to leave along with their flutes and lyres. She, for one, could not believe it. He was telling the mourners to leave!

The widow would stand to this effrontery. She would interrupt her wailing to exclaim to him, "Sir, I am a widow of

Israel." With what authority she held forth. "And on this day
death has come to this house. Apparently, sir, you do not fear
death. The Most High will strike you!"

To this the man answered with his own quiet authority,
"Widow, I fear death as much as anyone. Yet this is not death.
What we see here is sleep. The girl sleeps and needs to be
awakened because the wedding day is tomorrow and it must
not be delayed because the Most High our Father has cut short
the time. I have come to awaken those who sleep against the
day of the Most High our Father."

This had been the right move, for this sentiment the
widow understood and she immediately lent her support to
him. Relinquishing all her reservations, she stood with him as
he spoke to the corpse.

"Awaken little one!" he said, as if he were only rousing a
sleeping girl, "your wedding day is at hand."

The widow was a quick learner. She added, "Yes! It must
not be delayed, for the Most High has cut short the time."

In a moment the still eyelids of the corpse fluttered and
white cheeks became pink. Life returned. The bride awakened.
The man and the widow each took the girl by a hand and
presented her to the groom.

Before the widow could speak a word, the man had turned
and departed, saying to the father as he passed back into the
street, "Give her something to eat. She will need strength for
marriage." A bowl of thinly sliced apples and cheese was
produced. The widow raced to the man and said, "I understand about the time being cut short. Blessed be the Most
High."

"Yes," the man answered. "Blessed be the Most High our
Father. He raises the dead, for the time is cut short."

The mourners were then paid. Payment was not necessary,
they explained, not in these joyful circumstances. Still, the
family preferred to pay them. This was a poor family and
could only afford to give the widow two thin coppers. With
them in hand, she took her leave. With the two coppers she
could buy supper again this night and not return empty
handed to her kin. Still overwhelmed by events, she returned
to the temple.

In the Court of the Women there was the usual crowd. Pharisees were there holding forth on the tradition and contributing their grand gifts to the boxes with flourish and fanfare. Did they know what she knew, that the Most High had cut short the time? There were pilgrims there who were completing their grand devotions. Did they know what she knew, that the Most High had cut short the time? There, too, were the poor who had little grandness in their lives. All they were doing was pleading with vendors to sell them a supper that they could afford. Did they know what she knew, that the Most High had cut short the time?

Advancing farther she noticed that a crowd had gathered around someone. Could it be? Yes, it was the same wonderworker who had raised the girl. What words of wisdom and life he spoke. She recalled how she had first addressed him. She stood there at the edge of those listening. He knew what she knew and he knew more. Apparently, he knew much more. She fingered the coins that had been given her that day and considered their promise of supper. She walked over to the collection box marked with a sign, "For the poor of Israel," and deposited them and then returned to the circle of listeners. She could not be concerned about supper, for the Most High had cut short the time. For still one more time she gave it all. She gave all she had.

The young restorer of brides heard the coppers fall into the box and looked upon this giver. Now it was his turn that day to receive. For he had been often tempted not to risk all, but rather to claim success and withdraw. Yet, he realized, this great soul was so convinced that the time had been cut short, that she would no longer think of her own needs. It moved him to know that there were many such great souls in Israel.

Now with her hands free of coins and of all other encumbrances, she entered the circle of those who listened in wonder to the words of the man. However, she could not stay there long. The next day there was a wedding to attend.

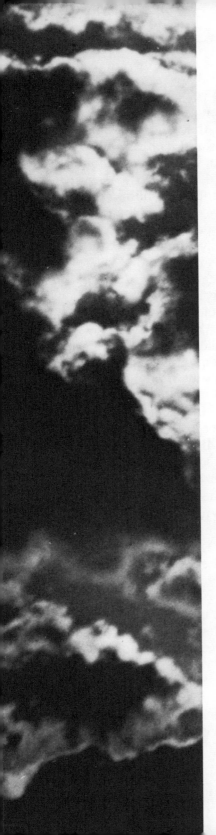

12

His Name Was Legion for They Were Many

"What is your name?" Jesus asked. "My name is legion," he answered, "for there are many of us."

(Mark 5:9)

All his townsfolk in Galilee whispered when they insisted that he should have never entered the army; or, in the least, not with such naivete about what it would be like. But his father had taken him into his hands at the hour of birth, the very hour of birth, and spoke as first words over him, "By Jupiter! One day may you command the legions of Caesar." From then on all expected that this would be his fate. From that moment of birth, it was inevitable.

Years later, at the time he presented himself for enrollment in the army, neither jaw nor tongue could be found in that town of Galilee that was not glib in approval of the plan. "Just like grandfather and father before him," they praised it. If there was caution, none of it was voiced. Duty and family honor expected that this son, at 16 years, would do what sons in his family had always done; that is, that he, too, would give both youth and courage for the empire and its mission. Perhaps, one day, as his father had sworn, he would command the legions of Rome.

In addition, it made sense for a gentile like him to join this gentile army. "Galilee of the gentiles" — that was the complaint that the righteous of Jerusalem made about the place. Yet do not be deceived, for in many ways this was not the case. True, Judaism was not yet 200 years old in the villages around the lake, but proclivities existing in every religion toward intolerance were present and lively already. Like in every town of Galilee, in his, too, gentile and Jew mutually disregarded one another. The military, therefore, offered a suitable alternative for a gentile in Galilee. As it was, there was not much chance for either advancement or success for him if he stayed at home. The military was a way of buying a way out.

As fate had it, his father would die in war. The rearing of the son, still only a young boy, then became the responsibility of the grandfather. Never did the grandfather fail to take advantage of an opportunity to impress upon the boy that it was for the sake of *pietas* that his father had made the sacrifice of his life. For example, on holidays, the grandfather wore the various decorations for bravery — crowns and necklaces by which the empire had rewarded both his and his late son's dedication.

The boy would ask, "My grandfather! Why is it that during the great festivals you dress yourself in these tributes and awards?"

The grandfather would answer, "It is because of *pietas*, my son! For there is nothing greater than love of empire and its society. Know this: your father had *pietas* so rich and abundant that he thought it a privilege to die for the empire. Though your father loved you, he loved the empire more. He would want you to have *pietas*."

Though it was a long time since he had been a boy, the soldier remembered this instruction. When there were only ruins of the soldier's life left, all jumped to the agreement that the pursuit of the family career had been a mistake; for, surely, it was obvious now, his composition had been too sensitive, simply too delicate, for the ruggedness and vulgarity of military living. Again, and it is right to inquire, why was not this sage counsel forthcoming while he was being supplied with heavy woolen tunics and fitted for the leather cuirass and shoulder pieces of the infantry? No, then there had only been the acclaim: "He is like father and grandfather before him."

Clues had been ample. For example, when young he had planted and tended a vineyard. This required both patience and dedication; not extraordinarily common virtues in "Galilee of the gentiles." This was the kind of sensitivity he possessed. Once an unexpectedly dry season had doomed the vines to certain death. During that whole time while the plants were frail and struggling, like a woman, he carried jars of water to them on a daily basis. That season the vineyard was saved.

As the vines matured, he carefully pruned. He understood how the correct use of small ropes promoted growth, corrected bushiness and created the strong vine that grapes required for development. Under his care all prospered. Later, while in the military, he would think of the vineyard.

His new life as Caesar's soldier had begun well enough. Though the period of initial training was severe, he made friends with whom he shared the hardships of forced marches, weighty gear and poor food.

Later, when that phase had been completed, he received his assignment. He was selected to be a bowman for Caesar. For this more training, long and arduous, would be required; but, since his station during battle would be in a chariot, he would be saved from the lot of the infantryman, from long marches and hard battles.

The training began in a prestigious camp that Julius Caesar himself had dedicated. The commander was a centurion who had been decorated for valor many times. He was legendary, for even though he had lost an arm in battle and had been given the opportunity to retire, he chose instead to command this camp where he could instruct soldiers in the art of the bow. Yes, *pietas* like his, everywhere to be found among citizenry of the empire, was what made Rome different from the rest. This *pietas* had already esablished the empire as one destined for life everlasting, world without end.

On formal occasions the commander wore the wreaths and armbands by which the empire had in years and battles past praised his bravery. Across his chest, too, in a harness, were the nine discs of honor, each with a name recalling a place of battle. They were reminders to the empire, not to him — he did not need to be reminded — of bravery done and duty fulfilled. Yes, he was admonition to the cowardly and preceptor for the young.

The daily regimen of the camp was arduous routine, for archery was a difficult skill to develop. For this young soldier each week of training witnessed improvement. While at first he could not even strike the target, as the days of training progressed, accuracy and speed with the bow improved.

Vines of discontent, once having taken root in his soul, now developed. While it was daily business for Caesar's soldiers to threaten mutiny and rebellion, the problem with his attitude was more subtle. It was not that days were long, packs heavy, and targets distant. His concerns were more nuanced. The fact was, he could not be a soldier. Something prevented him from being one.

Didn't soldiers reduce everything to a matter of dirt? Life was dirt over which to travel, dirt to be cleared or conquered, dirt for which to be fought, and upon which to bleed and upon which to make others bleed with more ghastly profusion. What counted for victory? Was it not blood upon the dirt? Could he explain this to anyone? Could anyone dissuade him of this?

"Best to dismiss these thoughts of dirt," he served as his own counsel. "Best not to try to explain."

Later on, he would point to this reluctance as the beginning of the darkness that would eventually consume his sanity. For these doubts became more and more deeply rooted. It would have been better for him if he had allowed them to surface at night before the fire or in the morning as grain was cooked over hot stones. That would have been better than having this dissatisfaction unexpressed in his stomach. Perhaps he would have discovered a kindred spirit there among the others. Perhaps among them there was another who understood.

He studied the centurion who wore the red cloak. He studied the centurion, who though he had only the one arm, was complete with *pietas*. The young soldier wanted to be loyal to grandfather and father. He, too, loved empire and yearned for *pietas*, for rich and deep *pietas*; but he experienced it as difficult. For, and this was strange to understand, he also wanted to be loyal to the vines which he had planted once and long ago in Galilee, in "Galilee of the gentiles." For him, it was Galilee of the vines. For there earth was more than dirt. The purple earth was fruitful like the womb and alluvial in its richness. Of this bad and enlarging spirit, the spirit that made all loyalty a thing difficult, he told no one.

One incident augmented his dissatisfaction with the army and convinced him that he was not a soldier. It was a small matter that would have been regarded as insignificant by nearly all, though not by him. At the time he had advanced enough in skill to begin learning to shoot from a moving chariot. On this particular day he had been ill and sought permission to return to the tent which he shared with eight others and fetch his brown cloak. His cloak was not red but brown, for he was not an officer. To his request, the centurion was not sympathetic. In fact, he ridiculed the request. Worse, he demanded that the young soldier ride in the open chariot, through cold, raw rain, and shoot five times as many arrows as the others.

"In war," the centurion growled, as if to provide rationale for cruelty, "there will not be time to return to a tent for woolens. Young soldier, it is not *pietas* to be sick. It is *pietas* for you to be strong for the empire. Your father had *pietas* unto death. Did he whimper with every sneeze? By Jupiter! You bear his name. Do you not want to be worthy of it as well? One day do you not wish to be worthy of his medallions, of his necklaces and his discs of honor and distinction?"

Comrades encouraged him to dismiss the incident from his mind. In fairness to his obliging spirit, that is what he tried to do. For a while he managed; but, as in most things, it was easier to forget at first; but, then after a short time had elapsed, the memory of it returned with fuller force. It was Satan growing in voice and volume within. There were times that it so weakened him that he could not lift his arms. Now again, he made an error in judgment. For deprived of peace by this, he merely said, "Best to sweep away this devil. To think is not too wise." Here again he served as his own counsel.

How Satan was making him victim of his wiliness. Herein was Satan's treachery: for a while the ignoring of these thoughts worked. For a while the soldier found it easy to be strong. This would last only for the moment. Comrades praised him for it. He himself was deceived into thinking for a time that he had succeeded in sending it forth from him by sheer force of intention. Only days later the memory of it returned and when it did, it was with multiples of its first power. Forget not the loneliness of it, for no one knew of this darkness. He would be fine for a while, tranquilly fulfilling his responsibilities, only to have it return. During any given night he would awaken to remember himself shivering in the chariot while the centurion urged upon him the *pietas* of his deceased father.

Once at home during winter leave, his grandfather told him a tale of how he had struggled in the military and survived because of *pietas*. Little could his grandfather have known that it was not the story the young soldier would profit from hearing at the time. In fact, it served to make it worse.

This had occurred while the grandfather had served in a legion of Caesar that had been placed at the disposition of Herod the Great. The king had entered into one of his insecure frenzies which was satisfied only by a river of blood. Herod had been told that a rival to his throne had been born. Herod, never one to hesitate, decreed: "Let all male children not yet of age three perish by the knife."

The grandfather, on duty in Bethlehem, was assigned to assist in the collection of these innocents. An informer told him about a young couple in a cave whose male child, having been born less than a week before, had not as yet been circumcised. There was something compelling about this new life and the uprooted condition of the parents that begged for mercy.

So, heedless of the risk, he advised them.

"Flee! Flee this place," he said. "The life of your newborn is endangered."

His action had been noticed and reported to his seniors. For this, he was severely punished. His punishment? He had been required to return to his own home and end first the life of his youngest son and then that of his daughter's son. Yes, he was told, "Caesar requires you to end twice the life you saved."

Thus did the grandfather reveal to the young soldier that both his uncle and cousin had died by his grandfather's own sword because Caesar would not be disobeyed, because it was required that twice the blood be shed that had in mercy been saved; and, last of all, because it was *pietas* to be obliging in spirit and not merely in deed. The young soldier's reaction to the story? Though not much registered on his face, the hearing of it devastated his soul. And his response? Silence was his response. More silence and breeding now in multiples of power, more satans.

It was during the same home leave that he visited the vineyard, the thought of which had often lifted him during the severity of military obligations. Though kin and townspeople had promised him that they would tend to it with the same care that he had, they had failed in their promise. He was appalled by the sight of it. Wild boars had gorged on its fruit; and what they hadn't ruined, thorn bushes had dominated and choked.

The soldier, devastated first by his grandfather's revelation and then by the sight of the vineyard, returned to finish training. Soon he was sent into battle. Though the others grew impatient with periods of waiting that preceded any action in the military, any action, that is, from battle to supper, the young soldier was patient. He was more occupied with the satans that kept returning in multiples of power.

Again an incident aggravated his condition. Once after a lopsided victory over a poorly defended town, this young bowman had been on the detail assigned to salt the fields of the conquered, for this territory which Caesar had won that day was fertile land. War exacts its price and even the dirt upon which this enemy had depended was now to be scourged. It would be years before crops could prosper again and before children could have grain for porridge. He did what he was told and explained to no one how within it was like Satan pouring salt upon his wounded spirit.

Though he became quite expert with the bow, when he was sent, as he often was, into battle, he was not prepared for the trauma that every warrior is called upon to bear. In battles he killed many, for now his eye was swift and his arm was strong. At first he told himself that these casualties were not men like himself. No, none of them had ever had a vineyard or a grandfather; more arrows from the sling. No, none of them had ever spaded ground or had been discouraged by the persistence of weeds; more blood upon the dirt as arrow upon arrow hit the mark. No, none of them had ever tossed a kid sister high through the air and then, as if surprised, caught her; more open bags of salt, pouring freely from the side of his chariot. Fields, already hallowed with blood, were now hallowed by salt. Always, he was his own counsel.

If only to someone he had confessed it all, maybe the multiplying satans would have stopped. Even for this it was nearly too late. He had always wanted to be obliging. He had wanted to succeed. He had, more than anything, wanted *pietas*. To march and fight for Caesar under his Roman legion's emblem of a pig was every meaning of family and honor. But to those who watched and worked with him, his external actions did not suggest that within destruction swirled in ever-increasing circles at the deeper level. For to them, he was a soldier, only a soldier. He was one like them, or so they thought.

One winter Caesar had no wars to wage and these soldiers were quartered in a monastery near the Salt Sea that was inhabited by desert monks. What contrast the soldier thought. The white robes, bleached by prayer and celibacy, worn by these bearded monks, were far from the leather cuirass, stained forever it seemed with blood and salt, in which this clean-shaven soldier of Caesar was dressed. While monks had the Holy Spirit, soldiers had *pietas*.

Throughout his time in the desert the satans returned with

greater turbulence. He slept poorly and often not at all. Once he rose early in the night, and, walking across their compound, entered the building that served as their chapel. The darkness inside it was so perfect and the silence was so complete, so comprehensive and absolute that the young soldier was startled when he realized that even one other person was there with him in the room. That he would not have even known if the singing had not begun. He could have left and would have never known that the chapel was filled with monks in bleached robes.

They sang psalms of mercy and of apocalypse:

> Let God arise, let his enemies be scattered,
> let those who hate him flee before him!
> As smoke disperses, they disperse;
> as wax melts when near the fire,
> so the wicked perish when God approaches.

> But at God's approach, the virtuous rejoice,
> exulting and singing for joy.
> Sing to the Most High, play music to his name,
> build a road for the Ruler of the Clouds,
> rejoice in the Most High, exalt at his coming (Ps 68:1-4).

Yes, they sang psalms of mercy and of apocalypse; and the soldier, who had poured blood and salt upon the earth, who had always served as his own counsel, would have been glad for either. That is what he thought as he listened to celibates sing under a canopy of night and stars, as they enhanced and did not break the silence.

"This singing," he thought to himself, "could only issue forth from hearts that are pure and pasts that are innocent." Perhaps it was not yet too late. Perhaps if he spoke to one of these monks, different from him though they were, it would help. No, in the end he decided that he would not. For one more time he served as his own counsel.

He had never confided to anyone the burdens of his own heart or of his own past. More devils and more satans with their multiples of power came. Now they rapidly approached majority within him. He had been an easy mark for them. That night there had been already so much of them in him

143

that he had been driven to roam in search of stars; and, if a soul like his from the Galilee of the gentiles could say it, in search of mercy and of apocalypse.

Still in the monastery chapel, he listened carefully to the choir. The singing, simple in melody and confident in rhythm, first soothed and then lifted him in a way in which he had never been raised before. Yes, while these monks had the Holy Spirit, the only spirit he had were the satans who, the more he swept them away, the more deeply he subjected them to his pursuit of *pietas*, the more and more they returned, in multiples of domination and control. After that winter garrison in the monastery, military duties were harder. An end was near.

One morning shortly thereafter they could not wake him. In his place in the tent they found him cold and gray. If it were not for his faint breath, they would have taken the soldier for lifeless. His was only one action: he endlessly counted on his hands with his fingers as if he were trying to reach some fantastically high cipher. For a week they watched him. They were confused.

Then because it was time to break camp and meet the enemy again, the centurion made a decision.

"Prepare a wagon and deliver him home to his grandfather," he said. "Too bad. He had a career before him." The command was carried out.

The grandfather wept at the sight of him. "Perhaps he needs long rest," the grandfather hoped. Others anxious to comfort him agreed. His soldier grandson required more than long rest.

Once home, his health continued to worsen. Though the coldness and the patina of gray left him after a few weeks, still he did not speak and still the counting on the fingers continued. In addition, now his manner became violent. While it was one thing to overturn and break jugs in his grandfather's cupboard, it was quite another when he climbed stairs that led to the rooftop and began to throw objects at passersby below. That provoked alarm throughout the village. As soon as this started, the will of neighbors prevailed to have the soldier confined on an embankment above the lake.

There were caves in the area and there he could be protected from causing harm. So one day men carried him on their shoulders to the caves. Though it meant more tears for his grandfather, they regarded it as the only solution.

The seclusion and peacefulness of these caves would have been the desire of the monks whose song was of mercy and apocalypse, but the soldier was wholly deranged. He was deranged with anger and with hurt, with sorrow and most thoroughly with guilt. In this state of terror, he entered into the deepest state of self-pity. It was mourning for the vineyards and gardens that were no more in the spring, for weeds, like satans, had grown there in multiples.

The sight of him was wholly pathetic. Now in the area of the caves, he paraded from time to time with a curved branch in his hand, thinking, onlookers supposed, that he was still an archer. Then at other times he imagined that he was in a town, dressed in military finery, bundling on the back of a passing Jew his heavy sack of entrenchment tools, baskets, mess dishes, ropes and stakes, and forcing the encumbered Jew to carry it the distance of a mile, the maximum distance which a soldier for Caesar could require of a son of the Most High.

At still other times, those who watched him thought he imagined he was in battle, loading his bow; and, thanks to the training of the valorous centurion, hitting the mark; that is, striking a chest over the place where the heart was and always with deadly, literally deadly, accuracy. After all, training in that prestigious camp which Julius Caesar himself had seen fit to dedicate, had been so fine. Then he was riding in his chariot, pouring salt from bags over the wall into the no more to be fertile soils of enemies of the empire. Dirt and blood, salt and war; it all was seen again in pantomime. They had been enemies only because they were in the path of Rome's desire. It deranged him further to think that there could be no more wheat for the children and no more husbands for the wives. Even now, still he was a soldier under orders. This time, though, it was legions of Satan that commanded him. He, who had never really spoken, still maintained fierce silence, giving up even the illusion of coping that conversation among the common provides.

Near this high embankment a gentile kept a herd of swine. Only in Galilee, "the Galilee of the gentiles," could that situa-

tion be tolerated. At night often the soldier's sleep was interrupted by the squealing of these swine. In his state of half-
sleep and half-consciousness, the soldier saw flashing before
his eyes the emblem of Caesar's legions, the pig, under which
he had served. Now it was not the stately and dignified pig
that smiths had with no small artistry hammered on Roman
shields. No, his sleep was tortured with visions of swine
whose mouths dripped with blood and salt. The eyes of this
herd pursued him in his dreaming; and, so fierce were they,
that even the contempt of a Jew for these pigs would have
seemed modest and a feeble passion against his contempt for
them.

At night then, while the still air carried sounds, in the
village below the embankment, the silence ended and his voice
was heard. He moaned, "Stop torturing me!" The torture
continued. Guilt and derangement continued.

Each day townsmen arrived with food, but even toward
them he became increasingly violent. At last they prevailed
upon the grandfather, "Hear us! We will not return to him, no,
not for one more time, until he is constrained." The grandfather agreed to confine the soldier with a collar. This would be
different than the civic collar which the grandfather wore to
commemorate bravery done for Caesar. There would be no
pietas in this collar. This was an accommodation for safety, for
the young soldier's safety and for the safety of the men who
would not go there, no, not for one more time, unless con-
straints were in place.

The collar wasn't strictly confining. They had attached it to
a long leash so he could roam. They hoped it would save him
from plummeting over the embankment.

However, they discovered the collar did not much help.
Throwing himself into frenzy, it seemed his strength increased.
Yes, it seemed that he had the combined strength of the devils.
The collar was easily dispensed with by his hands, and he was
free again to continue the grotesque parody of his prior life.
Again the men came and the collar was upgraded to ropes that
confined the hands and boulders that were attached by chains
to the ankles. Now in his froth to release himself, skin and
flesh were scraped and broken.

This was the prevailing situation until the day when the village, gentile and not Jewish in orientation though it was, was visited by Jesus. Hearing of the sad case, Jesus announced that he would visit the pathetic soldier in whom Satan lived in such evident force. While the soldier had the name of Caesar branded on his arm, Jesus had the name of the Most High writ upon his heart. In Jesus the Spirit lived in evident abundance. For them to meet would be a contest between the names, and between the spirits.

At the approach of Jesus, the soldier immediately took the offense, thinking that the first one to speak the name of the other would be the winner of this duel. That is how it would be in this war, in this war with neither benefit of chariot nor of arrows, a war with only the weaponry of names.

The soldier, his chin white and dripping with foamy saliva said, "I know who you are! You are Jesus. There! I have said your name! You can no longer trouble me! I say it again. You are Jesus!"

Jesus was placid, as if indifferent to the revelation of his name. Responding, he said clearly and distinctly, "Come forth! Empty his spirit of you. Come forth." If Jesus knew the name, he was not saying it. "Come forth now," was all he said.

To this offensive, the soldier countered, "Jesus! You are Jesus! Jesus!"

The Spirit within Jesus was greater than the spirit that had multiplied within the soldier, perhaps because the Spirit within Jesus was one, while the spirit within the soldier was many. Whatever the reason, the naming of Jesus by the soldier, however often it was repeated, had no effect. Jesus remained intrepid.

"Come forth!" Jesus said again.

The time was now at hand either for mercy or apocalypse. "Jesus! Jesus! Leave us alone."

Again Jesus said, "Come forth."

Then the soldier stood still, realizing that even though he both had known and spoken the name of this other, still, he was not able to conquer him. More was needed than the name. The duel was finishing. Now, in ultimate revelation of the superiority of the Holy Spirit, Jesus would demand to know his name.

"Tell me your name," Jesus required of him. "Amen! Amen! I say to you, if you tell me your name, the terror will end. I have come to promise you the terror will end. You can be emptied of them."

Then Jesus placed his palms under the cheekbones of the soldier's face and applied pressure. "The terror will end," he repeated again, "if you will but say the name. I require this of you. Say the name."

Jesus knew the name — that was because that much had been given him by the Holy Spirit to know. If he had been of a mind, he could have said it himself. Yet it was clear to Jesus that not he but the soldier needed to speak it. For it was the very essence of their authority within him that he had never spoken the name and that he had kept such silence. Though the pressure upon his face from the palms of Jesus was so vast that it seemed great enough in itself to evict the satans, still the soldier was silent, not yet ready to end this contest.

Then, in one abrupt upwards motion, Jesus flung the soldier's head so forcibly backward that it seemed for a moment that his neck would fracture. The soldier's reluctance ended as Jesus, for the first time, raised his voice.

"Do what you have never done," he shouted into the poor soldier's face. "Tell me now the name of the terror. I say, I will empty your spirit of it and send it forth into this company of swine."

The soldier looked over to the swine and in his mind saw once more the standard of the Roman army under which he had served. He knew that to say the name would take more courage than he had ever, even in war, displayed. For until now, this had been the soldier's whole salvation, however ugly a salvation it was, not to say the name, but to carry on in silence. Now Jesus, in whom the Spirit was one, was asking him to end the privacy and to abandon his every and single defense. He was requiring that the soldier no longer serve as his own counsel.

At last, he acquiesced. Falling into the arms of Jesus, he shrieked in a voice so piercing that all of the villagers assembled as they had on their rooftops to witness the duel, lowered their heads in pity.

"Legion is my name, for we are many." Those were his words. The soldier had done what Jesus had required of him.

With that it was over. He was free. He collapsed, unconscious. Jesus held him tightly to himself. Already the color of life was returning to the soldier's face. Jesus whispered, "Now it is over." The Satan that had grown by multiples of power had now been given leave. The soldier would never again need to count on his fingers.

But at that instant, the vast herd of swine squealed in one gross cacophony of concerts, as if someone with ten thousand arms had simultaneously cracked their hooves with as many thousand canes. They moved forward enfrenzied with fierceness that first seemed disoriented but then they were seized with direction. This did not end until they hastened over the embankment and perished in the great lake below.

It was just at this moment when, in that desert monastery near the Salt Sea, that bearded and white robed monks, celibate in their lives and prayerful in their ways, had gathered in chapel to praise the Most High. At the moment the soldier had at last been made empty, at the moment that the earth of Galilee, Galilee of the gentiles, vibrated with the stampede of cloven hooves, at that precise moment, their psalmody began:

> Break the power of the wicked,
> seek out his wickedness
> till there is none to be found!
> The Most High is king for ever and ever,
> the pagans are doomed to vanish from his
>   country (Ps 10:15-16).

The next day, the soldier was all dressed and clean and resting on his grandfather's rooftop. Seeing Jesus on the street below, he ran to follow him. "I will join your followers and go where you go."

This request Jesus would refuse. "No," he explained. "Your grandfather has suffered anguish enough. There is a vineyard here that needs to be restored. In the kingdom of the Most High our Father, many, many grapes will be needed."

13

On Sabbath the Man Born Blind Is Made to See

The man answered, "I don't know if he is a sinner; I only know that I was blind and now I can see."

(John 9:25)

On the sabbath all activity had to stop. Because of that, Friday was their hardest day for everything had to be done in duplicate. Twice as much water had to be carried. Casseroles were prepared for the next day, lamps topped with oil, and shutters tightly tied shut because a sandstorm might blow on Saturday afternoon.

The clever had devised ways of making life on Saturday agreeable. For example, many hired gentile children to arrive in their homes on Friday evening. These would light oil wicks and return the next morning. After milking the goat and feeding the beast, they would set

151

out a buffet for lunch. If you were fortunate, your sabbath helpers were industrious and your house would gleam more than ever by Saturday afternoon. Neighbors would boast to one another, "What worker bees we have hired." The Most High, ever pleased by cleanliness, looked the other way on the accommodations.

On one sabbath, while going to the temple for the observances, Jesus and his company passed a young man with a youthful face who had been born blind. Though early in pregnancy his mother had suffered a winter fever, no one made a connection. Neighbors interpreted the tragedy as moral: "Mother and father are sinners, and their sin is now paid by the child."

What suffering this young man had been made to endure, for he had lived with this judgment and gossip all through his dark life. Having learned the way to the courts of the temple, each day he sat at a different one of the gates with lyre on lap and he performed melodies of psalms, hoping that devout pilgrims or wealthy merchants would toss a coin his way either for his music or for his parents' sin. Personally, he could not have cared less either for the melodies or the psalms; or, for that matter, for the Most High before whom he would not bow. There was one thing he could see and it was this: he had been born blind with neither sin nor reason. But for the coins it was worth it.

The young man heard the crowd pass his way. Pilgrims were forever going up to the temple and he was not impressed by their piety. This crowd seemed to be more lively. Perhaps this day is a feast, he thought, wondering if one of the psalms was particularly appropriate. No, it was not a feast, he decided, just a crowd. More pilgrims, more coins, he thought. This would be a good day.

Then he heard a name. Jesus of Nazareth was among them. He had heard that name before. Prophets had passed by him often. For all their histrionics about the poor, it was none too easy a feat to wrench as much as one copper coin from a prophet. At least that had been his experience and he had been at those gates, a different one each day, throughout his dark life. Though he had heard this name before, as far as he was concerned, this man was merely the most recent in a series. One more crowd, one more name; that was all. Now, if Jesus would throw a few coins his way, that would be a different matter. Perhaps then, he, too, would become a disciple. The crowd stopped near the blind man.

One among them pointed to the youth whose parents had obviously been sinners and asked Jesus about his case. "Rabbi, tell us. Was it his sin or his parents'?"

The blind man heard this speculation and thought, Why this is none of their concern. True, he might have been born to sinners and for that, blind; but he had not been deprived of his power of speech. He advised the crowd, "Either give me your coins or move along with your piety, onto your altars, O righteous Israel! Do not stand idly near me. Remember, my parents are sinners. Perhaps I am one too. You would not want a son of yours to be born blind or leprous on account of your contact with me."

Jesus decided that the question deserved a response. "No! Neither sinned," he answered. "The Most High our Father does not strike us, however great our sin or innocence, with darkness. The Most High our Father is light and I am the God-light of the world."

Then, to validate the boast, Jesus spat on the earth, disregarding the sabbath proscription against the act. With fingers, then, he made a muddy paste of his creation. He continued; more spit, more fingers, more mud. The crowd stood silently, with heads down, half in reverence, half in apprehension, for the sabbath was not being observed. The blind man's face, however, turned upward toward the sun, which, of course, he could not see. For some time Jesus continued to spit into the small hole he had carved until a substantial amount of mud was at hand for whatever use he intended to make of it.

When he was done, he began applying the creation mud with four fingers to the blind man's face and head. First, he daubed it across each eye. The blind man felt the pressure of fingers and the coolness of the mud. Then the fingers went along his forehead, streaking his cheeks and the whole of his face with mud. Again the blind man lifted up his head and Jesus spread mud over the area of his throat and the back of his neck. Upon the long and not much washed hair of the blind man it was spread.

Jesus spoke to the man who had been born blind, saying, "You have taken all this mud, my friend. Now you must return it to the Most High our Father. Go now, blind man, and wash yourself clean in Siloam."

The crowd was astonished. First, it was the sabbath, the day on which though it was permitted to walk to the temple for the observances, it was not permitted to spit, to smear mud either across, along, over or upon the face of another, as had Jesus. Another feature was indefensible. It was not permitted to command another, as Jesus had, to break the sabbath's precept of rest. There could be no denying that Jesus had directed the blind man to go and wash in Siloam.

Siloam was a pool on the western slope of Mount Zion, formed at the end of the canal fed by Gihon spring. Now the mud man, with stick in hand, left the gate where he had been sitting and found his way along the street, in an unsabbath-like fashion. The sound of his stick tapping cobblestones and scraping sides of buildings, interrupted the pious silence of sabbath morning. En route, feeling the new sensation of light pierce the caked mud, his pace quickened. Soon he was careening down hilly streets and through narrow alleys toward the pool at unsafe and excited speed. It was awkward. Speed made the mud man clumsy. He tripped over stones and met trees and gentiles head on, as he followed the way to Siloam that he had memorized long ago when as a boy he had gone there to swim and not to wash. Seeing the blind man turn a corner at a furious pace, one smart goat leapt from his path, wisely, and not a moment too soon. What noise, though, he created. Hearing this racket in their darkened rooms and on their breezy rooftops, pious sabbath keepers whose parents had not sinned and who all their lives had been able to see anything they wanted to see, were outraged.

"As if his blindness is not sin enough," they exclaimed. "Now hear him ruined with strong drink on the day of rest, destroying the prayerful atmosphere of the sabbath in which we are trying to instruct our young. Apparently, this sin will surely come to still another generation."

But the mud man was making progress, considering that he was blind and caked in mud and repeatedly tripping over himself with excitement. The sensation of light continued to pierce the dry mud. Still, there was one collision after another. Mostly though they were with gentiles who were not as quick or as smart as that goat, to jump from his path.

Next, came the splash. It was such a full and complete sound that one who heard it might have thought a man had dived from the parapet of the temple, throwing himself successfully into deepest waters.

"Well," said one whose prayer had been disrupted by the racket, "he has found Siloam." Another added, "May that cold water sober him, and sober him perhaps, may the Most High be praised, about his sin as well."

Knee deep in Siloam, the man rubbed his eyes vigorously with water. He saw. He saw the muddy water as it fell from his face and discolored the clear waters of the pool. He washed his entire face.

Yes, he saw. For the first time, he saw. The blue and clear of the water he saw. Colors of mud and of sky, of fields and of earth, he saw. Looking at the sun, he squinted and wondered what that fierce color could be. If there had been fire at Siloam, he would have, for the first time, seen the color of fire, too. Mud man, blind man, irreverent man, could now see.

Once again, a peaceful sabbath had been broken, for as the seeing man saw his reflection in the surface of Siloam's water he shouted. Hitting the water in excitement, the image was broken, but his sight did not disappear. And that, too, made him laugh. For a while he played at it. First he would allow the image on the water to form itself. Then, he would strike the water with his fists and watch the image break.

So much for peaceful sabbath that day in Jerusalem. No, many were sure, Moses would not have been pleased. So much for the indictment of his parents' sin.

After a fashion that righteous observer had been correct when he heard the splash. Yes, the young man who had been born blind was appropriately sobered, but he was sobered first with eyesight and then with the Spirit. On Sunday, the day after the sabbath that had been so thoroughly ruined, his vision was the talk in Jerusalem and across the breezy roof-tops.

They said to him, "Tell us now how all this has happened. We want to know."

But his explanation did not help. In fact, it sounded only like so much mud and so much spit. Indeed, upon hearing it, they became afraid for it seemed that it was Satan who had put his fingers to these eyes and not the Most High. "Better let the Sanhedrin examine this case," they decided. They were so sober.

So, the entire story, spit and all, was rehearsed again in a chamber in the Hall of Squares before a quickly assembled portion of the Sanhedrin. They, too, were alarmed; in fact, so alarmed that they sought an assembly of the entire member-ship.

Then someone, having considered every angle, raised the possibility that this man might be an impostor. In other words, this could be someone's twisted notion of a joke, or an effort by one of the disciples of Jesus to embarrass the temple and its institutions. "Just like him, first, to pretend someone is blind, then to fabricate a cure. How convenient. What poor judgment to have done it on the sabbath. Let us not be naive about the view of the sabbath that his action suggests."

Good sense prevailing, this suggestion seemed worthwhile pursuing. So they subpoenaed his parents and interrogated them as well.

"Tell us," they demanded, "is this your son?"

"Yes, he is our son," they said.

"Are you certain?"

"Yes, we are certain. Each one of you in this high court are fathers of families. Is there one among you, even one, who is not able to identify a son? Of such a thing it is easy to be certain."

The questioning continued.

"And this man, the one you are so certain is your son, was he blind from birth?"

"Yes, he is our son. Yes, he was blind from birth. No, we cannot understand how it is that now there is sight where before there was blindness."

Though pressed harder in further questioning by the elders, the parents' story held, even though they were afraid. Having recently finished paying their taxes, they did not want their home and flour confiscated as penalty. So they would not testify one more word about this son who was now responsible for their great suffering for a second time. Their final words to the elders were, "While he looks young, he is, in fact, of the legal age Moses prescribed for witnesses before this body. Ask him for testimony. Let him who has sight now have voice as well." And, with those words, they left the hall.

Yes, the full Sanhedrin was required. Once assembled, the man appeared before them. He told the story again. But at this narration the Sanhedrin became hard minded.

"This is preposterous," one exclaimed. "Who would spit on the ground on sabbath but Satan?"

If slapping your thigh was one of the 39 actions proscribed for the sabbath, they reasoned, surely spitting on the earth, not once, but, as Jesus had, over and over, was an act heinous before the Most High.

Now their dean intervened. "Remember," he said, "it is like Satan's cleverness to deceive with an act of mercy." To the dean all listened carefully.

He continued the questioning. "Well, friend," he began. "Each and every one among us in this exalted hall rejoices with your good fortune. We have all heard the story. We have but one question. Tell the Sanhedrin, friend, what do you think of this man. Is he a sinner?"

Now the man had only been with sight for a day, but that was long enough for him to have decided that there were some things, like the Sanhedrin and its dean, that he could do without seeing. He answered with a stream of fire in his voice, "I was blind and now I see, and you inquire if he is a sinner? Your Moses should have been a sinner like unto this man. Then today your people would still not be in slavery." Now he was angry and perfectly indifferent to the scandal his words were provoking. And scandal he raised, especially the remark concerning father Moses and the continued slavery of the people.

With each narration of his story, the man became more

spirited. Again, something new was occurring within him. It seemed now that the healing had not ended with the Saturday bath in Siloam. His faith, which had been as dead as his cornea, was being restored. Though he had been indifferent to the psalms and the melodies, now his heart was coming into the fullness of light. The vision which he had received, however remarkable, had not been an end in itself. It was a sign that pointed to an altogether more remarkable quality of sight, more comprehensive than the gift of light bestowed upon his poor eyes, poor dead-from-birth eyes. This light was goodness and courage. This light was energy and strength. This light was the Holy Spirit. Could this be what Jesus had meant when he said that he was the God-light of the world? This the people did not desire to hear. Odd, but now it seemed to the man that they were the ones who did not want to see. They did not want to see either truth or light. Forcibly, the clerks who guarded the door led him out.

He left the court and the elders. He dismissed himself from all of them and their petty way of reckoning. It made little difference to him what their conclusions were. Outside there was daylight, and, of this one truth he was certain, daylight was too precious to waste by being shut indoors with the likes of darkness. Of darkness, he had enough. Anyway, he thought to himself as he walked away from them, there was one small matter to be completed. He needed to use his new sight and his old hearing to locate this Jesus, God-light of the world, the one who had accomplished this justice for him.

It was the God-light who found him. Now the man looked with eyes and with the Holy Spirit for the first time upon the one whom he had first known when he was in darkness and bitterness.

He said, "Sir, I did not know you when you spit over and over on the earth and then with fingers daubed first my eyes, then my face, my neck and my hair. Even now I do not know you. But even if you had not healed me, even if still my eyes were as blind as these stones, these stones of the temple, some polished and cut, some shaped like diamonds and others like ovals, still in you, sir, I would believe."

This was a man who had never bowed to the Most High because he believed that his parents were not sinners and no one had been able to convince him of the justice of his affliction. Now willingly and with conviction the man bowed low before Jesus, the God-light of the world. Even if the injustice had not been reversed, it would have made no difference. He still would have bowed to say these words, these words of light and justice, these words as bright but not as severe as the color of the sun, "Sir, in you I believe."

14

The Messiah Begins the Purification of the Temple

In the temple he found people selling cattle and sheep and pigeons, and the money changers sitting at their counter there.

(John 2:14)

Ascending the temple staircase beyond the Beautiful Gate, he recalled the first time he had gone up to Jerusalem from Nazareth to see the greatness there. First it had been to a holy city, then to a holy mountain, and finally to a holy stairs, all the while mother Miriam and father Joseph, at either side, held to his hands. At times the throng was so vast that he thought his parents would separate him in two, so severely was he stretched. Even though father Joseph and mother Miriam were connected to him at either hand, parents and son had become lost to one another once for three days. Levites had discovered the boy and cared for him in their barracks.

161

The three climbed the stairs and then father Joseph kissed him, for it was the first time son Jesus had climbed the temple. The boy wept, and who would not, as his parents sang with other pilgrims:

Acclaim the Most High, all the earth,
serve the Most High gladly,
come into his presence with songs of joy!

Walk through his porticos giving thanks,
enter his courts praising him,
give thanks to him, bless his name! (Ps 100:1,2,4).

The height and splendor of the place were vast. The excitement and joyfulness of the throngs were vast. Most of all, crowdedness for these feasts of the Most High was vast; so vast, in fact, that Sadducees had the saying that though there was not space enough even to press one finger between these people, still never did anyone complain that there was not enough room in Jerusalem for all who wanted to partake in the joy.

Priest merchants were everywhere engaged. As butchers, they carved meat that had been offered at yesterday's twilight before the altar. Young or impoverished priests could find adequate housing in temple dormitories. Throughout its courts, and in its many booths, priests sold salts and grains, spices and fig cakes, jewelry and aromatic unguents and butters.

Again, Jesus remembered his first visit. "No sound of hammer was heard all during the building of the place," father Joseph had said, passing on the story to still one more generation of Israel.

The father of Jesus had labored there during its construction as a carpenter. His fast eye and steady hand had served him well. While it was one thing not to want to leave Nazareth, it was quite another to be realistic. Besides farming, there was no work to be had in Galilee. A man needed a trade. For a project as vast as the temple, builder Herod needed many skilled laborers. While only priests, that is, sons of Aaron, would be eligible to construct the sanctuary of the new temple, there were rooms and corridors in abundance that were in need of Joseph's efforts. For that, no special lineage would be needed. It was enough to be a man.

So Joseph traveled to Jerusalem, as had thousands throughout Galilee. He came to build a temple for the Most High and for Herod, to line walls with panels of cedar and lay floors with juniper planks, to work in labyrinthine corridors and many rooms, but never to serve in the sanctuary, for Joseph was a son of David and not of Aaron and only priests could serve in the building of the sanctuary.

No denying, the temple was splendid for eyes, nose and ears. Admittance to its many gates, passages and elevated rooms was decided by detailed regulations laid forth in the law. Its maze of corridors and columns led inward and upward from the sprawling Court of the Gentiles, accessible to the public, to the Court of the Women, beyond which only male Israelites could progress. At the next elevation was the sanctuary reserved for the priesthood; and, at last, was the ultimate, the Holy of Holies, a cube of a room, layered with gold and embroidery, and entered only once each year by the high priest on the Day of Atonement.

Now Jesus was a child no more. He had been there for some days, participating in the sound and movement that never seemed to come to term. He heard the Latin, Greek, Aramaic and Hebrew that were spoken. He saw how from jerkwater towns and hamlets rabbis would join the caravans of their people for the pilgrimage that the poor could afford to make only once, if ever, during a lifetime. Jesus heard one rabbi say, "Keep the hope that during our pilgrimage we will meet the Messiah. If we sing fervently, perhaps the music of our hope will urge him to hasten."

Then psalmody, intoned with devotion that issued forth from a lifetime's hope, began:

How I rejoiced when they said to me,
"Let us go to the house of the Most High!"
And now our feet are standing
in your gateways, Jerusalem (Ps 122:1-2).

Jesus had arrived a few days before with the caravan from Jericho. Galileans, in the city for the feast, waited to welcome

him. Their ranks were swelled by Jerusalem friends and relations who had been made curious. It was the week of Passover, and, as he spoke to the people he seemed unexpectedly
well-disposed to the temple, to its cult and to its ethos of
clanging tourism and pious pilgrimage, on the one hand, and,
bustling commerce and political maneuverings, on the other. In
fact, he was there each day. At the first sign of dawn's light,
Jesus was in attendance for the prayers. With the rest he
heard, "Listen, Israel: The Most High our God is the one
Lord. You shall love the Most High your God with all your
heart, with all your soul, with all your strength." Again at
twilight he joined the assembly for evening sacrifice. He didn't
seem to mind the traders who made of it a market, the coin
changers that made of it a bank and the herders that made of
it a stable.

His behavior was observed. Could it be that this prophet
was at last realistic enough to admit that the temple and what
came with it was what made the big, wicked world go around?
At least that it made this world go around, this Judean world
that had succumbed for still one more time, like still one more
pawn, into still another foreign emperor's palm? No, surely,
nothing could have made Jesus that realistic. If he had so
changed, perhaps then there was still hope for this great
campaign of his which chronically seemed to be without focus.

"So he has learned something, has he?" many an observer
wondered. "This Judean world is not as weakened or as
unprincipled as he first thought," remarked another.

True, this Judean world held its breath for the time when it
would be a pawn no longer. While it held breath, it also
checked its ambitions, which were vastly pretentious. For none
on the face of the earth had maintained the aspirations which
these, who were so conversant with loss and devastation, had.

Judas, too, standing closely next to him, was pleased.
Perhaps, Jesus would admit that there was more to the temple
than met the eye. Could it be that in his newly found realism,
he understood that here was more than past and present.
Here, too, was the future.

They all knew what the past was. The past was adoption
and covenant, law and altar, promises and patriarchs. The

future in which this nation hoped enjoyed credentials equally impressive. For, in the future, theirs would be nations and wealth, lands and seas, scepter and hegemony over all. Had not that been the promise? Had not that been father David's vision?

Of this hope the temple was a sign, albeit one in stone and gold, cedar and jewels. It would be ready for service in the kingdom in whatever age it came. Its courts and columns, its altars and platforms, stood as both call and promise, as standard and inauguration. Did Caesar regard himself as imperious? This people could teach Caesar a thing or two, or forty, about being imperious. Apparently, Jesus was acknowledging this at last.

Earlier brusqueness had been a bad error on his part. Judas had made this point repeatedly. Had he been a bit more thoughtful, he would have forged an alliance with the Pharisees. They devoted their energy to the unity of their nationwide conference of synagogues. In fact, they looked on this temple as an archaic clinging to the past. "Let's not be more Jewish than father Moses who had no need of a temple," they cautioned. It was in this fashion that these two would promote themselves. Here again, Jesus had not been willing to meet them even halfway. Had he been, their support would have been forthcoming.

For example, Judas had persuaded the Pharisees to send emissaries to Jesus in Galilee. His hope had been that they would strike an alliance. Jesus made this the opportunity to complain about casuistry and hypocrisy, about the high volume of pharisaical prayer; and, imagine, about their broad phylacteries. No, Jesus would not suffer alliance with them.

"I swear by the columns of the temple!" cried frustrated Judas who had done his best arranging the delicate summit. Leave it to Judas to swear by the columns of the temple. "At one moment his vision is as expansive as the heavens. Then, the next moment, he can see nothing further than his beard. Let him give them their broad phylacteries."

Did it seem now that having failed in making allies with the lay Pharisees, Jesus had decided to cooperate with priestly Sadducees of the temple? "This will be a feat," Judas said to

Andrew. Judas was right, because for it to happen, Jesus would have to join in the refrain, "Blessed be the Most High for this house of worship, for it is a sign that Israel has not been forgotten."

Jesus would also have to look kindly on Herod, the one of late whom he had taken to call a fox. Yes, Judas plotted, that would be easy to finesse. "What the rabbi no doubt meant," he would declare, "is that Herod is as swift and as decisive as the animal."

The priesthood was friendly with the house of the Herods, insisting, "Give the devil his due." For however selfish his motives and however gentile his tastes, Herod the Great had built a new Judean world. Upon his roads the nation could transport grain and salt to bazaars. His waterways carried living water into the parched desert around Jerusalem. Could any deny that it was Herod the Great who had raised the temple, sign of the future that the faithful nation Israel was to receive? Yes, with the priesthood's positive assessment of Herod, Jesus would also have to agree.

In spite of what Judas perceived, Jesus had no fine esteem for this temple, for he remembered the prophets. The accommodating tribe of temple priests had contaminated the purity of worship, had repeatedly violated the law and opposed the preaching of the prophets. And, the temple endowment, gouged from the poor like mother Miriam and father Joseph, was more than once spent on bribery, or sent profligately to seal misbegotten alliances with weak princes. However, these thoughts Judas could not know, for Jesus was often silent.

Standing with Judas, Jesus observed a temple banker conducting business and exchanging coins. A slave stood on the auction block having only a moment before been sold for 30 pieces of silver, the price called for by father Moses for such a purchase. The man had been in great debt, and, even though he had wife and children, he chose to sell himself into slavery. The law provided that at the next sabbatical year he would be free.

The one who had purchased him stood at the banker's table, exchanging pagan silver for Jerusalem silver. Roman denarii or Greek drachmas, embossed as they were with human likenesses, were not acceptable currency with which to purchase a slave. Therefore they needed to be exchanged for Jewish currency, the half-shekel. On one side of this acceptable currency was the temple, and, on the other, names of father David and son Solomon. After establishing according to his own interests, a favorable rate of exchange, the high priest allowed for these pagan coins to be traded for Jewish; acquiring more denarii, heinous likenesses and all, for temple boxes.

Then Jesus observed ten men newly healed of leprosy making their way to the temple barber. Their disease had disappeared and they had come, as was prescribed by father Moses, to show themselves to the priests. After making an offering of thanksgiving, they were to receive ritual haircuts from a temple barber and thus complete their purification. Only these rites separated them from normal life. The barber saw them arrive, and, pleased at the prospect of afternoon business, sharpened a blade on a leather strop.

Next Jesus heard commotion. In their excitement, these lepers had arrived with no money and were told that they could not receive the purifying haircut. No shekel, no purity, that was temple policy. Lepers and barber argued. Then a temple priest came, and, no surprise, took sides with his clerical colleague. One of the lepers was pushed to the ground.

"Return back to your caves, rotting lepers," the priest cried. "Father Moses will not be bothered until you return with the prescribed half-shekel as the law demands."

Though Judas had tried to distract the attention of Jesus away from it, Jesus had seen it all. Then Jesus, who of late had apparently maintained support for the temple and its institutions, lost composure and ended his silence.

To the people around him Jesus said, "Remember these words of prophet Jeremiah: 'Put no trust in delusive words like these: "This is the sanctuary of the Most High, the sanctuary of the Most High, the sanctuary of the Most High." Amend your behavior and your actions. Do you take this Temple that bears my name for a robbers' den?' " (Jr 7:4-11).

Then, to barber and priest, Jesus said, "These men were lepers and they have suffered more than you or I ever will. The Most High our Father has seen fit to make them clean

167

again. Now you object that Moses cannot be bothered because they do not have the prescribed offering? Amen! Amen! I say to you, they have been purified beyond any authority that your razors or any privilege that your altars have to make clean. They are made clean by the Holy Spirit."

Then, gesturing to the temple, he said, "See this place, this pile of stone on stone, and of columns and pavements? Amen! Amen! I say to you, not one stone will be left. It is not these lepers, but rather it is this entire place which awaits purification. Who will have shekels enough for that? All 13 treasury baskets of the temple will not be adequate."

Like a torrent the words poured from him now. "Amen! Amen! I say to you, hear what I say, Jerusalem! I will tear down the walls of this temple which my father raised, and then I will rebuild them higher in holiness and more stately in righteousness in three days. Jerusalem! Await this act! Await a temple of mercy and of the Holy Spirit."

Of course, the disciples who listened thought that he meant father Joseph who had labored as a carpenter during the construction of the temple. They did not know that he meant our Father who is in heaven.

Next, grabbing rushes that were used as bedding for sheep that had been quartered there awaiting their Passover fate, he made a whip and scourged the clergy for the adherence to the law that authorized such cruelty to lepers rather than to the Spirit who authorized such mercy. Then before anyone knew, he went to the table where the banker was finalizing the sale of the slave and overturned it. The pile of pagan silver, 30 pieces high, fell to the pavement. The likenesses and insignia inscribed on them rolled across the cut and polished stones. Young children attached at the hand to parents were released in an instant to run free, joyous at their sudden wealth. Unknown to all was that before this Passover week was finished the same silver price for a slave would roll again across these stones.

Temple police, an extra cohort of whom had been laid on for the feast, arrived. With the help of Judas, they carried Jesus out from the court, his hands which that morning had orchestrated such disruption and trouble, were tied together with rope. Later Judas went to the commander of the cohort to make an apology and secure the release. He told the commander that this had been an isolated incident and that Jesus had been under great pressure. He found the official sensible and willing to understand. In fact, they had already untied his hands. One of the lepers had returned and was speaking with Jesus.

"We see his kind here every day," the commander said. "If you promise to keep him away from the courts for the rest of the feast, today's disturbance will go no further." Judas was grateful for the discretion. Jesus was free to go.

But there was one thing that the commander of the cohort did not know. It was the same thing that Judas did not know. In fact, neither that one leper who had returned nor the slave who was now free, neither the priests nor the Pharisees, neither the singing pilgrims nor the children who were connected, as Jesus once had been, to parents at the hands, knew. It was something only the Holy Spirit knew.

It was this. A disturbance at these quarters greater than the commander's augmented forces could handle was at hand. A disturbance greater than the spilling of silver or the chastisement of the clergy was at hand. A disturbance more profound than either war or the coming of spring was at hand. For from that moment the purification of the temple was at hand.

15

The Embrace of Friend Judas

Now the traitor had arranged a signal with them. "The one I kiss," he had said, "he is the man. Take him in charge and see that he is well guarded when you lead him away."

(Mark 14:44-45)

Now the long knives were drawn. Now the Jewish establishment could do nothing else but weigh out 30 pieces of silver and call for a quorum of their court, the Sanhedrin. Now at last they saw how they had underestimated the cleverness of this dangerous man.

How had he done it? That would be a question asked for a long time. Sensible people would conclude that it was a combination of both his words and his actions that had won him such power in the eyes of the people.

Now they admitted that Jesus was the master of word and story. At first they had taken little notice of him. His words were the innocent stories that he called "parables." Frankly, often they

171

didn't even make sense. At first hearing they seemed the most harmless of teachings; as harmless as a woman sweeping her house for a lost coin, as harmless as a father throwing a party for a returned runaway, as harmless as the tiny mustard seed that grows with speed and certainty.

Along with his stories were his actions, which he preferred to call his "works." They, too, seemed harmless, especially since the beneficiaries of them were those who had no power. Who would expect those ignorant of the law to organize a campaign to fulfill it?

His company of followers were utterly powerless. For example, he was popular with the sick. Wasn't ignorance of the law the reason for sickness? Every rabbi taught that.

Then he sympathized with gentiles. That surely was wasted effort. What knowledge of the law did those who were not children of father Moses have?

Next came children. Nothing would do but for him to lift children into the air. Children were of absolutely no importance; not until, at least, they could recite in the law.

Could anyone doubt why there was no reason for him to be taken seriously? He told little stories and made friends with those who had no entry either to the sanctuary of the temple or to the pulpits of the synagogues.

It would have been smarter for him to have aligned himself with those who knew the law: priests and Pharisees. From their stone altars and their elevated pulpits they could do something for him. These and not, as one phrased it, "these rabble who know nothing of the law," were the ones who could have forwarded his campaign; and, in return, he could have helped them.

Of late something new and dangerous seemed to be occurring. Could it be that all the harmlessness of his sayings and of his works had gained momentum? His parables were being retold over and over by others. With each telling they seemed to yield deeper understanding. At the beginning one of the Pharisees had come out to hear this great speaker of reputation, but all he heard was an afternoon of stories. He returned to his colleagues and reassured them that they had nothing to fear from a man whose teaching was only a string of, what he called, "dark sayings." Now they didn't seem so dark any longer. Their meaning was only too clear to any who wanted understanding.

It was something to see and hear. Little children were telling the parables to their grandparents. Mothers were telling them to their daughters; and slaves to their masters. Enemies were speaking to one another. The parables were spreading. The kingdom they proclaimed seemed to advance through the very telling of them. The lost coin was being found. Runaways were falling into their father's arms. The mustard seed was growing with speed and certainty.

Knowledge of his actions, too, was repeated and was now more difficult to discredit. "Yes, the man was blind," you would hear at the booth where you had gone to buy oil, "and the man touched his eyes with spit and mud. Then he could see."

"Yes, we were all hungry, for we had been there the whole day long," a woman says to another at the well in the morning, "and he gave us bread and fish to eat."

Or while freeing his nets from tangles, a fisherman could be heard saying to his brother, "I tell you, the girl was dead, as dead as dead could be! The next day she was to be married. They had dressed her in her wedding robes. He came and threw out the mourners and the color of life came back to her cheeks. 'Your wedding is at hand,' he said."

All Jerusalem now, crowded as it was for Passover, was telling the parables and rehearsing the works. The company that followed him, now swelled with sinners, gentiles and children, did not seem as harmless as it had earlier.

Yes, though they still had their altars and their pulpits, the priesthood and the Pharisees were now anxious. For it had been a long time since one of them had given a sermon that was even remembered, not to mention repeated as were his parables. It had been a long time since one of them had soothed a fever, not to mention raised the dead.

Now the long knives were drawn. Now they realized how clever this one had been. Hoping that it was not too late, they decided to take their losses with the people and cut him down. Weighing out 30 pieces of silver they would silence this teller of parables and stop this worker of wonders. They all admitted that his stories and his deeds were fast throwing everything in their marble world of altars and elevated pulpits, their world of delicate peace with Rome, off balance.

No, they could not blame themselves for having waited too long; for, at the beginning, he had seemed only harmless. After all, weren't the stories that he called his parables innocent? Weren't his actions on behalf of those who were ignorant of the law that he called his works harmless?

They were glad for it when Judas chose to cooperate. They were not surprised. After all, Judas was the only one not from Galilee and therefore not wholly one of them. It was merely a matter of time, everyone believed this, before the support for Jesus would divide and the center of it give way. In fact, someone described Jesus pleading with them once after still another of their frequent internal disagreements. He sat them down and put a child in their midst, a child so innocent and free of the tangles in which they had enmeshed themselves, that, for a moment, they were startled. Then putting his hand on the child's shoulder, Jesus said to them, "In the name of this child's innocence, I plead with you: the support cannot be divided."

Though the campaign was gaining in momentum among the people, in the center of it, that is, in the company of the twelve, there was trouble. If the support was to be divided, it was no surprise that this one, Judas, would be the first to separate. After all, he was not from Galilee. He was not wholly one of them.

The officers of the Sanhedrin were pleased when Judas chose to cooperate. The high priest was informed, and he, too, was relieved. They would need this help in order to know precisely where Jesus could be located. Since their arrival in Jerusalem days before, whereabouts of this band had been unknown. Even with Jerusalem streets and passageways illuminated by the brightness of this paschal moon, still at night darkness was everywhere and it was forbidding. Obviously, the Mount of Olives, the place where he sequestered his disciples most of the time, was extensive. Would they be able to locate him in this or in that grove? Would it be here or there? At what time would he make an appearance?

Earlier they had sent their best, their fastest, and their most erudite questioners to him in Galilee. They tried to entrap him in his own words, but Satan had made him too clever for them. His nimble tongue had outmatched theirs.

Herod Antipas had had enough of him and ordered him out of his Galilee. Hearing of his compliance, Herod Antipas laughed with self-satisfaction, "So this prophet is not too brave after all. He knows that Antipas never makes a boast which he will not fulfill. He has not forgotten the baptizer John. I beheaded John. Now Jesus is in Jerusalem and he is Pilate's problem." Between Herod Antipas and Pilate there was neither love nor friendship, at least not yet.

In Jerusalem, the Sanhedrin was more concerned than Pilate. They had no patience with either this problem that Herod had deported, or for his kingdom which was, quite frankly, hard to envision. Actually, he was all of Jerusalem's problem. The place was tinder. Everyone knew that. If Jesus incited rebellion, Rome would crush Judea as if it were a flea. Though Pilate was not naive to this, still, he would never act to put him away. So, it became more imperative that other authorities take the initiative.

The day after the arrival of Jesus the high priest abandoned even the semblance of nonchalance and dispatched the temple police with instructions to arrest. Claiming to be amazed, however, these returned without him. "No one has ever spoken like that before," one said. This was something incredible. They returned without him. "This is not going to be easy, after all," thought the high priest.

And Satan had made him difficult to spot. First, Jesus would appear in the precincts of the temple, teach outlandishly, damage the piety of the faithful and then flee from the city, probably to nearby Bethany, there to take shelter upon the rooftops of supporters. "Some Jew he is," one criticized. "Days of Passover are at hand and he does not even sleep in Jerusalem."

They could no longer risk the mischief that he was capable of stirring, and the rebellion he was capable of igniting. For example, immediately after his arrival he had come to the temple. It was at the time of Passover, height of pilgrim and tourist season. He mounted his high steed of righteousness. With a whip, he interrupted the commerce and economy on which his beloved poor depended. Yet never once through his campaign had he suggested a better idea, another way or a new system. Was he losing his mind? That is what kin in Nazareth had feared. That day in the temple his own disciples had to take him away. If a Pharisee had with whip and all, done what he had done, or, if one of the temple curia had, do not doubt that he would have had things to say. "See their violence," would have been his cry. Wasn't he the one who had said, "Turn the other cheek?"

Yes, best to bring him in and end the whole matter swiftly. Nothing to be gained by delay. Given this man's personality and potential for mischief, it would be the wisest of all possible options. Though it was neither official nor legal, still and all, a small discrete group of "citizens" — armed citizens — would be the most advisable. Everyone would understand and, in fact, be appreciative. Now how helpful of Judas to be willing to betray the whereabouts, for a fee, of course. That was no problem though, not for this temple and this treasury.

They would take custody of Jesus and bring him to the high priest, who would hastily convene an executive committee, a prudently selected executive committee, of the Sanhedrin. One could be sure that they would not hesitate. A swift verdict would be reached.

Someone had already been to Pilate. He was ready to play his role. How frustrating Pilate could be. He was reluctant to promise anything to them, but, as long as his meddlesome wife did not interfere, Pilate was tentatively willing to have his cadre carry out the dirty deed of death, in Roman style, that is, by crucifixion. While bloodly crucifixion was not exactly the sort of function that enhanced the holy days, neither did this man's teaching nor did the dangers he posed enhance Israel. Now this Judas was in their circle and, as such, he was in the perfect position to know where Jesus could be found. He was their treasurer. He would betray the whereabouts. Then at an opportune moment and in discrete fashion, he would signal the "citizens" and make the identification. He suggested that he accomplish it with a kiss. "Best for me simply to approach him and offer him the kiss of a disciple. That will be your sign." A kiss. How droll. What a fine touch.

Yes, crucifixion was the cruelest method, but given the potential for trouble that was at hand, it was a larger mercy for the nation. If there was any question, it would have to be explained as that. No, there wouldn't be any trouble, not if they were careful.

High Priest Caiaphas was not wrong on this. "Better for one man to perish," he had said, "than for the whole nation to be lost." He was not exaggerating. Everything was at stake.

In the gardens on the Mount of Olives the citizens awaited him nervously. This group would be different than the one who had gone earlier and returned impressed and empty-handed. One of the temple police was now the commander. He was a young officer who played his part to perfection. He had excelled in his training and was thought to be the best. He was going places in his career. Privately, in the living out of his life, he knew how to enjoy himself; but publicly he was always correct as befitting someone of rank in the temple establishment. Later he would recall that this had been the strangest detail he would ever command.

At last Judas arrived. He came to the young officer. "We have just kept Passover on a rooftop in Bethany. They are still singing the psalms. Shortly they will come to a grove not far from here. Yes, I am certain of the location."

Judas was depressed on Passover wine and somewhat dejected over the deed he was about to perform. Still, though, he was willing. He had gone this far. Silver jingled in the bag attached to his belt.

"We must act quickly," he insisted to the officer, "for he knows something. As we reclined at table he said that one of us would betray him. Then, I cannot have any doubt, he gave me the evil eye. Yes, he knows. Yes, some of the rest are suspicious of me. They always have been. How did I respond? I quickly promoted Simon as candidate for traitor. 'Why, that stumbler,' I muttered to his brother Andrew, 'he's capable of accomplishing such a shameful deed by accident.' Andrew can do without his brother. It was easy to convince Andrew."

Then with Judas who had just received, he was sure, the evil eye, and the young officer, the correct one who, though he was going places and highly regarded, was sure always to have his time at the lead, the "citizens" moved to the grove where the betrayal was to occur. Their numbers were swelled by Pharisees and priests.

Yes, as Judas had assured, the group of them were there. What could be better? With the exception of Jesus, they were asleep. Only Jesus was awake and pacing through the columns of olive trees. At moments like these, if Jerusalem could see him, they would know that he was not supremely confident.

"The one I shall kiss is the man, seize him," Judas said to the officer. Then, with lips like ice, Judas came to Jesus, and putting his face to his, kissed him. "Rabbi!" he said. With the word, the deed was finished.

The "citizens" did their work. Judas had been right, it had been the evil eye. Yes, Jesus had known. No, he was not surprised.

"Friend, you betray me with a kiss?"

The sleepers heard the commotion and stirred. Thomas roused them and they rushed as a group into the grove. The silver of Simon's sword flashed beneath the light of the paschal moon.

"Simon," prisoner Jesus lamented, "you have been the first to shed blood this night."

16

A Hasty Trial

The chief priests and the whole Sanhedrin were looking for evidence against Jesus, however false, on which they might pass the death sentence.

(Matthew 26:59)

Though all regarded the style of the young clerk announcing the arrivals as overdone, this young student was sure that only high drama was befitting an occasion of this importance. "From the synagogue of Macedonia," he proclaimed, "the servant of the Most High and father of a family of Israel, Hezron."

It was the task of this clerk to announce names and districts of the membership as it arrived and to keep the count. "From the synagogue of Maritima in Phoenicia, the servant of the Most High and father of a family in Israel, Jehoram."

A quorum needed to be established before the proceedings could commence in a lawful manner. "From the synagogue of Caesarea in Gaulantis, the servant of the Most High and father of a family in Israel, Daniel."

Not until the minimum number of 23

had arrived could the trial begin. "From the synagogue of Arimathaea in Judea, the servant of the Most High and father of a family in Israel, Joseph."

Now they were entering the hall in numbers. "From the synagogues of Gadara, Tishbe and Gerasa in the Decapolis, the servants of the Most High and fathers all of families in Israel, Saul, Jehoshaphat and Isaac."

There would be no problem reaching the necessary number; not on this day, not for the spectacle that was about to unfold. The counting of the elders continued. "From the synagogue of Aenon near Salim, the servant of the Most High and father of a family in Israel, Nicodemus."

Word had gone forth to the whole membership of the Sanhedrin on the day before to be prepared to assemble at a moment's notice in their temple chamber called the Hall of Squares. The arrest was imminent.

The Sanhedrin sat by the gates of the city by the bridge over the Tyropean. Part of the hall was within the sacred enclosure and part on non-sacred ground. "From the synagogue of Capernaum in Galilee, the servant of the Most High and father of a family in Israel, Michael."

Outside, the faithful awaited the first light of day that would signal the beginning of their prayers. It was barely daybreak when the 23rd arrived. Yes, this deliberation would be lawful. The clerk would summon all the intention he possessed. Standing, he faced the two presiding officers of the Sanhedrin. The Nasi, that is, "the prince," was an elected president, and the Abh-Beth-Din, that is, "the dean," was the most senior member of the court.

"O lawful prince! O lawful dean!" he proclaimed. "Twenty-three elders of the nation are in attendance before you and thus the prescribed quorum. All is as father Moses required."

"Moses, indeed," whispered one reluctant member of the quorum, the one from Arimathaea. To the man next to him, Nicodemus, he remarked, "this will be a farce."

Joseph of Arimathaea would be right. For if anything then, if anything before then, or if anything come after then was *fait accompli*, it was the outcome of this assembly. For the high priest had already decided. Wonder of wonders, he had already arranged for Pilate's support. During the night that had preceded this dawn quorum, while these fathers of families in Israel slept, while pious wives of Israel on this night before Passover scoured pots and pans to purify them of any leaven, an unlawful band had taken its prisoner. On this night, in disregard of all the provisions of the law which they held so stoutheartedly, against all the traditions of their nation, and against the least requirements of justice, an unlawful band had taken its prisoner. The mob that had taken this man into custody could not pretend to claim any subpoena. Now before High Priest Caiaphas Jesus would appear for preliminary, though, in fact, as they knew, summary judgment. Remember, it was Caiaphas who had said, "Better for one to die than for the entire nation to perish."

The Sanhedrin was in order. During the next few minutes nearly all of its 71 members would enter and pass the clerk at the door. Since the session was convened, the clerk could no longer trumpet the arrivals with a flourish; unfortunate for the clerk who enjoyed this task.

The purpose of this assembly was largely cosmetic. After going through the motions of a hearing, they would ratify the decision that the high priest had made during the night. Yes, it had been decided. The prisoner was to die. But the order of events that would lead to that was now a cause of speculation. The law did not permit them to put anyone to death. For this, swift action on the part of Pilate would be essential, absolutely essential. No telling what would occur among the people if Pilate delayed execution after the Sanhedrin had passed its verdict of guilt.

The prisoner was conducted into the court and the trial began. More than tired, he appeared hungry. As a first-born, he had fasted the days of Passover to commemorate the many first-born who were slaughtered in the plague against Egypt. The effects of the sleepless night and the days of fasting were manifest in his face.

The testimony of at least two witnesses would be required before the Sanhedrin could recommend the death penalty. It is prescribed in the law: "A man may be put to death only on the word of two witnesses or three; and no man may be put to death on the word of one witness alone" (Dt 17:6).

The witnesses were also to be men who were free and healthy in sight, hearing and speech. They were to be adults. Neither women, children, slaves, deaf nor dumb could testify. Why? These were notorious liars.

The first choice as witness was a young man of considerable wealth. There would be no problem with him. Apparently once, in all sincerity, he had gone to Jesus, and confessed that he was desirous of eternal life. With his typical offhandedness, Jesus told the young man to rid himself of wealth and scents, of property and wardrobe, and follow him penniless, landless and in shabby attire. Foolishness! Here this young man, willing to make his considerable resources available to the campaign, was dismissed abruptly. The young man turned to the high priest. Now Caiaphas was no fool. He opened before the young man, shall we say, a wider gate to eternal life. Yes, the young man, in his finest robes and scents, would be only too pleased to testify against Jesus.

The second witness would be a disciple of Simon the Pharisee. Remember, it had been at Simon's dinner party that Jesus had preached his gospel to a prostitute. Simon was a man of position, status and leadership. For the benefit of others he often reviewed the many responsible positions he had held. Who was this Jesus to withhold his obeisance? Now all Jerusalem was questioning Simon's capacities. Simon would wait forever, if need be, to take revenge. He had nothing better to do with his time. Simon trusted that if he were patient there would be a chance.

After these witnesses had been selected, they were instructed so that their witness against him would appear in exact agreement. Testimony was required to agree in detail. If it did not, it would not be admissible. In fact, if they were found guilty of perjury, theirs would be the same punishment that had been intended for the accused. Since the case against this man involved a capital offense, if their words succeeded in convincing the court, they would have a part to play in the actual enforcement of the sentence of death. The thought of that had sobered many a witness since the days of Moses.

This day the witnesses had been thoroughly trained; as a matter of fact, their testimony had been written by none other than Annas, father-in-law of the high priest. Annas did not want his annual rival for the throne of high priest, Boetus, to have any reason to criticize him for the fashion in which this delicate affair had been handled. Caiaphas could not be certain where the forces of Boetus stood on this matter. It was troublesome, any way one approached it. The night before father-in-law Annas had said to Caiaphas, "This man is enough to drive Pilate and Herod into one another's arms." Yes, it would be delicate.

The law tilted in favor of the accused. For example, when a sentence of death was handed down, two more than absolute majority were required. In addition, the delay of an entire day was required. During this the Sanhedrin was to engage in both the prayer and fasting intended to further sober their judgment. If the verdict was unanimous, the sentence was deferred. The person was acquitted, because, and this was the reckoning of the law, it was presumed that only prejudice could have accounted for a unanimous verdict.

Before the witnesses testified the oath was administered. This was solemn business, too. This the clerk accomplished with vigor.

"Do you swear to tell the entire truth?" he questioned.

"I do so swear," the witness answered.

"Do you swear to tell the entire truth, by the Most High and by heaven?" the witness was required to answer.

The witness said, "I swear to tell the entire truth by the Most High and by heaven."

"And by Jerusalem and by the consolation of Israel?" the question was posed, now with more detail and more force.

"Yes by that sacred place and by that great sacred hope."

For still one more time the clerk administered the oath. "And do you swear to tell the entire truth by your children and by your share in paradise?"

"Yes, by my children and by my share in paradise. I do swear it. I do so swear. By all this and more I do so swear."

The first witness came forward. "Yes, I know the man. Yes, I have seen him on many occasions and have listened thoughtfully to his teachings. I heard this prisoner say, 'I am going to destroy this Temple made by human hands, and in three days build another, not made by human hands' " (Mk 14:57).

After he left the room a second witness was ordered to enter. He, too, was given the oath. "This will all be over in a moment," thought the high priest confidently.

The second witness proceeded to offer testimony to the Sanhedrin. "Yes, I know the man. Yes, I have seen him on many occasions and have listened thoughtfully to his teachings. I heard this prisoner say, 'I have power to destroy this Temple made by human hands, and in three days build another, not made by human hands.' "

The high priest acting as if scandalized by these revelations, turned to the prisoner and said, "Listen to these charges. Seize the chance to defend yourself. Speak! Speak on your own behalf! We are here for the sake of the truth. Inform us in the truth."

But the prisoner said nothing. Apparently that morning he did not sense much of the spirit of the truth in the Hall of Squares. His silence aggravated the high priest.

Joseph of Arimathaea had listened carefully. The law was clear. Testimony needed to agree in detail and already there was discrepancy, and only one discrepancy was necessary to invalidate testimony.

"So," Joseph thought, "the high priest cannot even teach two men to memorize the same script. 'I am going to destroy' is far different than 'I have power to destroy.' "

Then the servant of the Most High and father of a family in Israel, secret disciple of prisoner Jesus, Joseph, decided that while he was willing to forfeit reputation, lands and position over this, he was not willing to lose soul. Standing to speak, he relinquished all — all, that is, except his soul.

"We all know that this testimony cannot stand before the Sanhedrin," Joseph argued, "it is conflicted. It is not in agreement and therefore it cannot stand."

Though the high priest had noted the discrepancy, he was stunned by the engagement of Joseph. Having come this far, the high priest was not about to allow the conviction of the prisoner to slip through his fingers. He wondered why he had wasted his time on this nonsense about the dismantling of the temple in the first place.

Allowing Joseph's objection to stand, he opened a new charge. "On to the more substantive accusation of blasphemy." He would attend to Joseph's gross disloyalty at a later time. Turning once more to the prisoner, the high priest asked: "Tell this assembly, are you the Christ, the Son of the Blessed One?"

At last this was a question the prisoner chose to answer.

"I am," he said. "And you will see the Son of Man seated at the right hand of the Power and coming with the clouds of heaven."

Against all the provisions of the law of father Moses which regulated how a prisoner was to be treated, the clerk, who had to this time been so mannered and polite, even as he gave his vigorous performance, stood and slapped the prisoner broadly across the face. The high priest ignored this. Considering the prisoner's words, he thought to himself, "This will do just fine."

Then gesturing with his hands in a grand way, grand because it was meant to reflect how grieved all Israel was, the high priest stood and tore his robe the required length, that is, the length of a man's palm, saying as he did so, "The Sanhedrin has heard the blasphemy! The man deserves death. No need for a vote. No need for further witnesses. He has committed the crime of blasphemy and deserves death."

The Sanhedrin nodded in agreement. Jehoram agreed. Daniel agreed. Saul agreed. Jehoshaphat agreed. Isaac agreed. Hezron agreed and Michael agreed. The rest, too, agreed. Yet Joseph, the one who decided that though he was willing to forfeit lands and station, was unwilling to lose his soul, would not agree. Noting his abstention, the high priest was pleased and thought to himself that Joseph's action had actually served his best interests. Now the high priest could defend the verdict of the court because it was not unanimous.

"And from what district does he come?" he inquired.

Arimathaea was the answer.

"Oh yes," he knew the place. "He is the one with fine lands."

Joseph stood again to speak. He had a right to speak and no one, not even the high priest, could deny this.

"My points are three," he said. "The Sanhedrin holds that blasphemy, the charge against this prisoner, is as technical as it is weighty. For blasphemy to occur, the accused needs to have spoken distinctly the name of the Most High as it was revealed to father Moses. This, the prisoner has not done.

"Second, when there is evidence of blasphemy, it is the responsibility of the court to provide the accused every opportunity to recant. Friends of the court, who have not been apprised of the charge, are to examine the prisoner while the court watches to see if they arrive at the same verdict of guilt as the court had earlier.

"Finally, who has ever heard of an accused witnessing against himself, as the high priest has permitted this prisoner to do in our midst? Credit Moses for his wisdom. The law is so to prevent any possessed soul, with the aim of ending his wretched life, to enter such testimony against himself."

In the center of the tribunal sat two other young clerks with ledgers. One was to record all votes for acquittal; the other, those for conviction. The youngest of the court would be the first to vote. On this day, both clerks would leave without having made a mark, for the high priest had determined that no vote, neither of the youngest nor the oldest, needed to be recorded. Joseph's objections were not sustained.

Though the trial had not gone perfectly, the high priest was satisfied. Joseph, do not doubt this for a moment, would be appropriately sanctioned. But now there was not a moment to lose. It was in their best interests that Jesus be arraigned before Pilate immediately. For his appearance before Pilate, the charges would have to be altered. Pilate was not interested in executing a prisoner on charges of blasphemy. This man would have to be represented as a danger to the empire. Then Pilate would be persuaded. Then Pilate would regard it as his responsibility to authorize his execution.

So a fresh brief against prisoner Jesus was prepared. Now he was charged with disturbing the people, with condemning the payment of taxes to the emperor and with proclaiming himself king. With these charges, Pilate would have to cooperate. All depended on him now, for his alone was the right both to judge and punish.

The prisoner was led out of the tribunal through an assembly that, in spite of the high priest's theatrics and in spite of the clerk's solemn drama, had now fallen silent. The prisoner passed Joseph and stopped. He spoke for one final time in a lawful assembly of Israel.

"Councilor Joseph," Jesus said, "you have lost everything today for my sake."

"No, not everything, Rabbi," Joseph answered. "I have not lost my soul."

Then the prisoner remembered how he himself had prayed, "Not one of those you gave me have I lost" (Jn 18:9). And that was the final thought the prisoner had as he was moved from the hall where the Sanhedrin met. Outside it was morning.

17

Joseph Gives His Tomb

Then a member of the council arrived, a good and upright man named Joseph. He had not consented to what the others had planned and carried out. He came from Arimathaea, a Jewish town, and he lived in the hope of seeing the kingdom of God. This man went to Pilate and asked for the body of Jesus."

(Luke 23:50-52)

Little had Joseph of Arimathaea realized when he arranged for the stone-cutter a month before that first to be buried in the new tomb would be his name and fortune. As soon as colleagues on the Jewish council, the Sanhedrin, heard that Joseph had provided his own tomb for the interment of Jesus, and, with that, become aware of his silent discipleship, they would move to impeach him. That he might not return north to Arimathaea with funds in his belt, they would fine Joseph to the last coin of his wealth and to the final parcel of his land holdings, each of which was considerable. The wiser course of action would have been to dispose of this bag of blood in the trench where criminals were usually discarded. The vultures, who had neither coins nor lands to lose, would eat his flesh. Joseph preferred that Jesus be buried in a tomb.

In spite of the tomb's setting in a landscaped garden, the burial itself was the final indignity. The Romans had timed the crucifixion so that death would come by suffocation the same hour as Friday's sun was to set. Then the sabbath would have begun, the day, of course, on which there could be neither reverent washing of a corpse nor dressing of it with spices. Gentile teenagers would be engaged to carry the body to the tomb on a board of lumber. Descending the four steep stairs, they would crouch and turn sideways to enter the deep and narrow opening that led to the antechamber. Advancing into the second chamber, the tomb itself, they would set their burden on a ledge where it would wait for the sabbath to end. Then the last rites could be given.

As for most burial vaults, for this one, too, a limestone cave had been selected. This rock was soft enough to cut, yet dense enough to resist moisture. Enough niches had been hewn into the face of the walls of its burial chamber to accommodate Joseph, his wife and children, and any Arimathaean relations who would by chance happen to die in Jerusalem. Like all such tombs in Judea, its exterior was whitewashed so it could be identified at a distance. The law of Moses was explicit: even to approach the dead brought on defilement. Therefore, it was important for tombs to be visible.

Now it was Sunday and sabbath was over. Hordes of pious and devout Jews who had descended upon Jerusalem for the feast of Passover would this morning be returning to villages in Judea, Galilee and the Decapolis. The events of this Passover had been as exciting as they had been unexpected. For during the days that had preceded, Jesus had been taken into custody by the authorities of the temple. There had been a trial at dawn before the Sanhedrin in the Hall of Squares. Then, after the whole people had assembled in Pilate's yard and clamored for his blood, he had been executed.

It was still not yet dawn. At last the sorrowful were free to come to the whitewashed tomb with rolls of spice. There must be haste. Joseph had hired a new gardener and this was to be his first day of employment. He had instructed him to bring a mason to entomb the body with stones and mortar. "And have it done soon," he ordered, "before dogs come for still more indignity." These days, both in the Hall of Squares and on the hill of Golgotha, Joseph had seen enough of indignity.

The place was prosperous. The one who had called the poor blessed was buried as a rich man. The entrance was a spacious garden that wealthy Joseph had begun landscaping with dogwood, rose of Jericho and hyacinth, all of which now were in fragrant Nisan bloom.

Joseph's new gardener, determined on a good beginning, had arrived before dawn. Though he had wanted to begin the previous week, he could not since it was Passover. There was much to be done. Attending to his new responsibilities, he was grateful for the position that had been given. The gardener was still something of a novice at this work. He had served in Caesar's army for many years in southern Italy. Recently completing his years of duty, he was entering upon retirement now. He had chosen Jerusalem in which to live for here there were many other retired military personnel on the pension the empire awarded. His arm was marked with the hot branding by which, years ago, he had been tagged indelibly for service to the Caesars.

He thought it best to begin with the figs. Last autumn Joseph had his previous gardener plant a long row of tropical fig saplings here. At first, that man had been reluctant. "Figs are for tropical Jericho," he said to Joseph, "and not for temperate Jerusalem. Such delicate trees will fail if winter is not mild." Winter on mountain Jerusalem could be raw and wet. Though agreeing, Joseph still remained committed to the saplings. So, as precaution against the winter, he required the gardener to bury each one in the earth.

That had been an elaborate procedure. First, the gardener treated each tree with a generous application of oil. Then he wrapped each trunk and branch in swaddling strips of heavy wool. He finished the procedure by covering each with pelts from lambs that had been sacrificed in the temple. Finally, and this maneuver required caution, ever so gently, the gardener folded the entire tree over for winter burial in a shallow grave which had been dug. So it was that warm in their winter beds, these trees awaited spring. This week it would be the task of the new gardener to unearth and raise them all and to see if they had survived winter.

The gardener was busy about this when he noticed that during Friday's storm the ancient apple tree that stood in the corner of the garden had been struck by lightning. He had been told that the tree itself had long been regarded as useless. For a long time it had produced only bitter fruit. Though Joseph had pestered the previous gardener about removing it, there had never been enough time. Now Friday's lightning began the project. I will please Joseph, the gardener thought, I will take care of the apple tree today. Yes, the gardener decided to lay ax against that tree, and, once and for all, have it finished.

A woman passed him as she entered the enclosure. They noted one another. He thought she was a wailer who had been hired to raise a tumult at the tomb. She hurried past with great determination and looked indifferently at his efforts upon the apple tree.

"Friday's storm did this," he called out to her. "Wasn't it something! Its hot winds filled the air with sand and darkness in a moment. It reminded me of sirocco storms, the kind you have only in Sicily. That was no local weather." The woman, however, scarcely nodded in his direction.

Passing him, she proceeded toward the area of the cave itself. There, encumbered with towels, spikenard and linen dressings, she faced a detachment of Roman legionnaires encumbered with shields, javelins, and daggers. The week before had seen their convoy travel south from their legion's garrison in Caesarea to augment the single cohort usually in cantonment in Jerusalem.

Expect the Romans to be prepared for any eventuality, she thought. Engines of war! Engines of deterrence! Along the road they had wheeled stone-hurling catapults, state of the art for crowd control, expecting the worst from the usually intense Passover throng. She marveled. Even now, after everything was over, still the Romans were prepared. At the insistence of many, Pilate had been persuaded to station this detachment in the garden, to guard the entrance to the tomb.

"Best to be ready," they argued before Pilate.

"Ready for what?" the procurator asked.

"Ready for either dogs or disciples," they answered.

But it was still dark and the legionnaires were asleep. Only the commander and a sentry were awake. Actually, this had proven to be good duty for them. Not one had taken it seriously. For the soldiers it had not been a night of thieves or ghosts, it had been a night of too much wine.

Now she was upon them and would seek entrance to the area. According to their procedures, the sentry would conceal the daily challenge word in a sentence. This day the word was "sun." He asked, "Does Caesar's eagle look at the sun?"

Had Miriam known the counter word for the day she would have presented it then, as he had first presented the challenge word, concealed in a sentence. The counter this day was "dawn." "At night, the eagle of Caesar must sleep under the moon and wait for dawn," would have been an appropriate reply.

The sentry looked at her. One woman, obviously harmless, was no reason to alert the rest, he decided. She could pass this post without knowing the counter to the challenge. The commander, though, who himself had too much wine the night before, was feeling its mean effects and would have some ridicule for her.

"So," this newly promoted captain remarked at the sight of her passing the sentry, "only a woman of his is brave enough to come. Where is the company of stalwart disciples? But who am I to complain about cowardice?" he admitted, gesturing to his own sleeping minions, strewn like so much ruin around their camp. "You know, woman, Caesar's army could use someone like you. Too bad the emperor doesn't commission women. Go forth to your messiah if you'd like, though I am not sure your scents are needed, for there is not yet stench."

Then, remembering that the mouth of the tomb had been sealed with a large round stone, he hammered a shield with a dagger to rouse the detail. He ordered four to go with the woman to the tomb and roll away the stone in order for her to enter and be of service for a final time in the short-lived kingdom of Jesus.

To the astonishment of all, upon arriving at the tomb, they saw that the stone was not in place. True, they had been in a rush, but on Friday the wedge that checked the stone had been pulled out permitting the stone to roll forward. No small effort would have been required to roll it back. Who had been there earlier?

The woman remembered that on the day of death itself, there had been unexpected kindness from two members of the Sanhedrin. First, with great courage, Joseph of Arimathaea had gone to Pilate and petitioned that the body be released. Then he provided his own tomb for its interment. It was a new tomb, not merely one whose inner chamber had been emptied of old bones and of an old name. Then, Nicodemus had come immediately to the tomb and inserted aromatic myrrh and aloes into the cavities of the body. Could it be, she wondered, that either of these two had returned? If one had, the woman thought, it surely had been a night of too much wine, for none of the soldiers had seen anyone.

At the sight of the opened tomb, the captain became anxious. Not merely his new rank, but now his neck was in jeopardy. It was not common for the temple hierarchy and Pilate to see eye to eye on anything. Yet on the issue of the burial of this man, they had agreed. It was all to have been over now. There was to have been no afterlife for either this gospel or this man. Now the tomb was open. Taking a torch, the captain rushed into the entrance of the tomb and then further into the burial chamber. From within, Miriam heard him cry out to Jupiter. Yes, the body was gone.

"Stolen!" he cried, running in the direction of the centurion headquarters where he would make a hasty confession and initiate a hasty lie. Pilate, whose wife had been troubled in a dream about this man and who had been among those vocal ones pressuring the procurator to detail the soldiers in the first place, would not be pleased. The captain feared that this would go to legion headquarters; and, who knew, for it was serious enough, even to Caesar's legate for the area. He lived in Syria.

Taking the torch which had fallen to the earth, Miriam

entered the tomb and saw herself that the ledge was empty.
The cloth which had covered the body was neatly folded and
still smelled of the hundred weight of myrrh and aloes that
Nicodemus had delivered. The pile of rocks that had served as
a pillow for this deceased was undisturbed. She remembered
how once he had said that he had nowhere even to lay his
head. In death, too, she thought, they would not let him rest
his head, even on a pillow of rocks.

The company of disciples had to be told, she realized. She
would be able to locate Simon and John in the area of the
Mount of Olives. She would have to travel in haste for now,
with the sabbath ended, they would take advantage of the
commotion that attended the resumption of commerce to flee
Jerusalem. No doubt especially these two would seek refuge in
Galilee. She feared that she might be too late, for already
dawn was at hand.

She walked into the new light, in easterly direction, that is,
toward the olive gardens where they had made their camp this
past week of Passover. Entering the city through the Water
Gate, she passed into the upper district that was only beginning to show signs of life after this long weekend of both
festival and slaughter. She stayed with the streets as they
twisted and turned in many directions. They forced the traveler to pay careful attention. For a while she followed along the
same narrow street that Jesus had traveled on Friday. Her route
took her past the Antonia Palace. There she saw the steeds of
the detachment from the tomb already tethered in the yard,
wearing fine Roman blankets. As she quickened her pace she
realized that inside a newly promoted captain was making
nervous explanations. At the pool after the Sheep Gate she
turned into the area of the Mount of Olives, all the while
hoping that it was not too late.

She arrived at the grove where their booths were. She
rejoiced: though they were preparing for departure, Simon and
John were still there. As for the others, who could know where
they were? Likely, by now they were scattered through the city
and Bethany.

"The tomb is empty," she announced, "I went there early.
The stone was rolled away. First the soldier and then I went in.

The body is gone. It is not there. His mother should be told by you. More heartbreak for Miriam."

Simon said to John, "Let us go to the place."

"Be cautious," Miriam said. "Danger is everywhere. They will notice you as you pass through the city."

But even as she was speaking, the two had begun on their way. They ran through groves of olive trees, feeling their speed quicken as the earth dipped into the Valley Kidron. Then, across the valley itself, they stepped cautiously over its stones. Climbing its far wall, their speed declined as they ascended. The temple came into sight before them. John, younger and more vigorous, led the other now and determined the route. They ran through the temple promenade. The Golden Gate was above them at the next elevation. They crossed through the Court of the Gentiles, passing the Royal Porch and the Hall of Squares where the Sanhedrin had met. They had cut through the temple yard at this time because John thought that this would be far safer than going near Antonia and its military barracks; especially, if officials had already received the report of the empty tomb.

Simon's weight and frame made running difficult. Never having moved so quickly, he felt perspiration fall from his face and spread down from his neck. John moved ahead at a relentless pace, not yielding to Simon's slowness. Now they were beyond the temple and traveling through the city, squeezing past stalls and sellers, brushing against walls, passing those who merely loitered, those who, unlike themselves, had no urgency. The rich were carried forth on litters and others made progress on mules. Swiftly, the two passed all. Morning had come and the city was awakening to life. Simon crashed into vendors setting up booths at busy corners, selling final provisions to the caravans of pilgrims anxious to be on their way. They would be beginning their journeys home in a short time. The breakneck speed of John and the awkward, though persistent pursuit of Simon drew the attention of everyone.

Someone recognized Simon.

It was a young woman. She said, "Mother! Look, at that one running. He was one of them. I recognize him. He was one of them."

When John came to the place the guard had not yet returned. Staying in the garden area, he waited there for Simon. Shortly he arrived. The gardener who had by now started a fire to burn the fallen branches of the apple tree looked at Simon and then at John as he pointed in the direction of the tomb.

First Simon entered, then John. They did not speak to one another. However, they did not think of theft, instead, they thought of victory; that is, they believed. "This is the day the Lord has made," said John.

All the while the ax of the gardener was heard. They went past him again as they left the garden. Together they thought of places where the others could be located. They thought that all were still in the area, all, that is, except for Thomas. Neither knew where Thomas was.

They were long since gone when Miriam returned. She entered and examined the tomb. Finally, she thought that the gardener might have seen something.

Going to him she said, "Sir, if you know where they have placed him please tell me so that I may go there."

Then, laying down the ax, the gardener said to her, "Miriam."

With that Miriam knew and she too believed. She clung to his feet, but he would not have that. Instead there was work for her. She was to return again, through the courts and past caravans making ready for departure, along the alleys and stairs. Through an awakening Jerusalem she was to return and summon the Eleven.

On one thing the newly promoted captain had been wrong. For on this day this woman was indeed commissioned. Hers was rank higher than Caesar's adjutant could confer. She was commissioned to bring the news.

"I commission you," the gardener said, "to tell them to direct their steps from this city of brutality and travel north, there to the great sea, and to wait there for understanding and for resurrection."

Empty wine skins and dishes of the soldiers lay on the ground, as well as many of their provisions and gear. The captain had directed some to return and gather them. As she left, Miriam saw the detail arrive. On this day, nothing would be lost, nothing, that is, except, perhaps for the apple tree that during Friday's storm had been struck. Even that was all right, for its fruit had been bitter. Long had it been bitter, longer than any could remember.